ECONOMICS OF CONFLICTS AND RESOURCE CONTROL

BLESSING OKENINI

ECONOMICS OF CONFLICTS AND RESOURCE CONTROL

A ROAD MAP FOR REGIONAL DEVELOPMENT IN THE NIGER DELTA

Blessing Okenini

Blessing Okenini.com

FOREWORD

How could a people or nation continue to be and how could they survive the trials of the moment? To this initial question I respond: they must guard jealously the memories of their past. But how can people without a memory survive the trials and the tribulations of the moment? To this second question, I respond: in that case, a colossal work has to be effectuated; they must quickly retrace their steps, step into some residues of the past to reconstruct their history in dialogue with the present. For hardly can a people without a memory survive the challenges of the present. The present will always chastise them with its riddles and having no substance to fall on, the future will always elude them like a mirage, tossing them from one misfortune to the other, and all this in an indefinite vicious circle.

It is this colossal work that Blessing Okenini has effectuated for all of us, who – having found ourselves in the turmoil of exploitations that has characterized the economy of the Niger Delta and have no clue how we could survive the trials and the tribulations of the present moment – offers us not just a residue, but a substantial memory of our common past as a people; Besides, in this book *Economics of Conflicts and Resource Control*, our author reminds us of all the intrigues and the struggles that have surrounded the Niger Delta, abundantly blessed with natural and human resources. He launches us into the future, inspiring us, with this precious memory, to aspire to capture the future and make it a possibility, if we must continue to be a people.

Blessing Okenini is one who knows his onions: he is a qualified economist/analyst of international reputation. With a master's degree in Economics from the prestigious University of Pisa, in Italy, he has access to all the information required to bring knowledge to the limelight and make it available to all. As one who in Nigeria has worked at Chevron, Warri—which is at the heart of the exploitation of the Niger Delta region—he understands all the intrigues, all the struggles and challenges. As a fully-fledged Urhobo citizen, he, like the common citizens of that region, had experienced all the devaluations, sufferings and subjugations which have, even before the years of the Ogoni nine, oppressed all Niger Delta citizens and still cry for help till today. Thus, like one who wears the shoes, he knows how it pains.

I recommend this beautiful masterpiece of vibrant quality, not only to the Niger Delta and Nigerian citizens but to all people, insofar as they identify with the struggle for survival or have identified with such a history in the past. It is a clarion call for the international community too, to embrace the enriching information in this masterpiece as a guide in the quest for dialogue and a lasting conflict resolution in this marginalized part of Nigeria.

I read the book at one gulp and I have come back to it several times, as a reference point. The same could happen to you.

Ekweariri Dominic
Bergische Universität, Wuppertal, Germany

Contents

INTRODUCTION

The desires and aspirations of the founding fathers of Nigeria during the pre-independence era was to build a strong and stable Nigeria that would be established on the tenets and principles of true federalism. However, after a few years of independence, these desires and expectations turned into national confusion and crisis when the civil war (6th July 1967-15th January 1970) broke out. It is obvious that the agitation and clamour for the control of resources by host communities and federal units have been a major factor in the problems facing the Nigerian Republic. Significantly, the Niger Delta region's clamour and agitation for the control of their resources has escalated to another level of conflict.

In this book, which is a compilation of my findings, I try to argue that the failure of successive governments in the past to abide by the tenets and principles of true federalism in the spirit of equity, fairness and justice, especially concerning the control of resources, has been the sole cause of the various conflicts in the nation particularly the armed struggle in the Niger Delta.

I also try to examine the nature and magnitude of the cost of the oil-related conflict in the Niger Delta region. The cost of the conflict ranges from the loss of lives and property, negative impact on the welfare of the people, the reduction in oil production and revenue generation to insecurity in the region and arms proliferation. The methods and strategies that the government has been using to manage conflict in the Niger Delta region have proved defective.

An integrated bottom-top participatory process that is aimed at securing the quality of life of the people in the region and protecting the environment from further degradation is the only pathway to sustainable peace and regional development in the Niger Delta region.

CHAPTER ONE

UNDERSTANDING THE CONCEPT OF ECONOMICS OF CONFLICT

WHAT IS MEANT BY ECONOMICS OF CONFLICT?

In the past four decades, the interest and attention of social scientists and economists in the study of the Economics of Conflict and its resolution has been increasing. The desire to find out more on the concept of conflict prompts Economics of Conflict experts to embark on extensive work to consolidate their arguments on the subject. In their view, conflicts are of various dimensions and degrees. Conflicts can occur within a state as civil unrest, insurrection, terrorism, violence, crisis, agitation and struggle or it can occur between states as war or aggression on a definite territorial border of one state by another state for economic or political reasons. Conflicts can be in different forms. The failure to protect and enforce property rights within a community, state or nation can have adverse consequences on the economic activity and growth of that region and can degenerate to Economics of Conflict if it is not properly managed by the appropriate authorities. The government arises in the advent of a conflict to protect the property rights of a unit in the society in return for taxes to support its protection and other services that the government renders to individuals, communities, states or regions.

In this chapter, I examine conflict from an economic perspective which arises often due to property rights, agitation for control of resource ownership, uneven distribution of the wealth of a state or region, the exclusion of individuals, states or regions from the decision making process of an economic system and the insincerity of policy implementation that neglects the critical issues of individuals, group of persons or regions that are paramount to their existence. If resources are appropriated to a certain group of individuals to the detriment of others, the people that are neglected and excluded from the sharing formula can put up some form of resistance and the government may at a point, channel more resources into its military and police to put the resistance under check[1].

Resources can be allocated by government officials to subdue the people's resistance or to prevent their agitation from escalating. Game Theory, which has become an important tool in Economics in recent times, is used by economists and researchers of Economics to analyse conflict which occurs when economic agents oppose one another in an intense struggle and agitation over the control of resources, property and lives of individuals or groups of people in a region. Most economists used the Game Theory concept in their articles on economic conflict like the Nash Equilibrium; a position in which no player would have a consensus to change their strategy.

Conflicts may take different forms and may have a great influence on many areas of human activities. For example, labour market conflicts can be associated with strikes, labour lockout and employee-employer remuneration benefits. Conflicts can also involve litigation and legal manipulation over the disposition of wills

---

[1] Grossman1995

or property. Also, conflicts may include terrorist campaigns designed to achieve political objectives, including resource control transfer.[2] In each of these examples of various forms of conflict and struggle, the outcome is affected by a contest success function, which defines an appropriate outcome based on the "inputs" of the fighting effort.

In the past centuries till date, disputes and agitation over territories and resources are the primary cause of civil wars and conflict within a state or among states. I examine the effects of conflict on the economic outcomes, to determine the factors in which economic output is distributed within an economic system and how individuals', states' or regions' share can be correlated to its productivity.

ECONOMICS OF CONFLICT IN NIGERIA

Prior to the 1956/58 discovery of crude oil by Royal Shell company in Oloibiri, Bayelsa state, the Nigerian economy was based on Agriculture and was one of the highest exporters of palm proceeds, cocoa and other farm products in Sub-Sahara Africa and it enjoyed relative safety and peace at the time. However, after crude oil was discovered, the country has known no peace and has encountered all kinds of security and environmental challenges.

This book exposes the adverse impact of oil-related conflicts on the general economy of the country, the effects of environmental degradation on the health and livelihood of the people in the oil-producing areas; youth restiveness and civil unrest, and the proactive approach that the relevant authorities and stakeholders

---

[2] Enders and Sandler 1995

can employ to bring a lasting solution to the conflicts and how a sustainable peacebuilding process could be started in the region.

The discoveries made by the research in this book will be relevant to economic actors like the oil multinational companies, the oil producing communities, the various armed ethnic and militant groups and the government authorities.

This book addresses three critical issues:

i. The main feature and causes of economic conflicts in Nigeria with emphasis on the Niger Delta region.

ii. Roles of oil multinational companies in fuelling the conflict due to their method of operations in the oil-producing communities in the Niger Delta region.

iii. The weak political will of the government and her insincere policy implementation towards elevating the plight of the host communities.

Also, this book emphasises that adequate and timely management of economic conflicts, civil unrests and violent crises are major elements that must be incorporated into a broad framework of collaborative management of the multinationals and government respectively. Collaborative management becomes effective and efficient when institutions and processes that regulate resource allocation and usage are able to anticipate and respond to stakeholders' (host communities and ethnic groups) different interests over resource usage and can seek a solution to mutual benefits.

DEFINITION OF KEYWORDS AND TERMS

Here are some terms that have been used throughout this book and their definitions.

- **Economics of Conflict:** It involves competing for motives to attain scarce resources. Each party wants to get the most that it can, and the behaviour and emotions of each party are directed toward maximising its gain.

- **Agitation for resource control:** This is the arousing of public concern about the ownership and control of resources.

- **Youth Violence**: This refers to behaviour involving physical force, intended to hurt, damage, or kill someone or something for the purpose of sending a signal or call for attention.

- **Armed struggle:** It is the process of taking up arms as a means to achieve a goal.

- **Conflict management:** This measure is taken to limit, mitigate and contain conflict with the aim of transforming the conflict to lasting peace through addressing the root causes and effects of the crisis.

- **Conflict resolution:** This is the measure taken to address the underlying issues of the crisis and thereby enabling the parties to terminate the conflict and deal with the disputes through an open process of dialogue.

- **Conflict prevention:** This is a measure taken to keep a low-level of dispute from escalating into significant violence between parties concerned and to limit the spread of violence if it does occur.

- **Environmental degradation:** It is the diminishing of the environment's resources and the deterioration of their quality through air and water pollution, land erosion, the destruction of the ecosystem, animal extinction and desertification.

- **Natural resources management:** This is a system that monitors the extraction, use and trade of natural resources among numerous stakeholders including the individual consumers of natural resources, international institutions, businesses and industries, government, NGOs and local communities. Effective management prevents corruption, degradation and severe scarcity, and improves transparency and equity in the extraction and use of natural resources.

- **Natural Resources:** These are materials that occur in nature and are essential or useful to humans, such as water, air, land, forest, fish and wildlife, topsoil and minerals.

- **Resource-dependent economies:** These refer to economies that depend majorly on a particular natural resource where they generate their revenue e.g. (Nigeria-Crude Oil).

- **Exclusion**: This occurs when stakeholders are excluded or omitted from the natural resources management process. In some cases, local communities or individuals whose livelihoods depend on the extraction of natural resources may be left out in the management of the resources. In other instances, ethnic or tribal groups may be excluded in an effort to marginalise them politically or economically.

- **Environmental security:** This is the freedom from environmental destruction and scarcity and deprivation of resources.

- **Revenue:** It is the monetary value that is received from the trading of goods and services, including natural resources.

- **Resource right:** This gives the authority to mine, control and trade natural resources.

- **Peacebuilding:** It refers to the process of establishing sustainable peace by addressing the root-cause and effects of violent conflict

- **Stakeholders:** They are various groups such as the government, businesses, industries, landowners, unions, rebel forces, international corporations, organisations and NGOs that have an interest in the extraction, management and trade of natural resources.

- **Sustainability:** In the context of natural resources, sustainability refers to the harnessing of natural resources without depleting them. It can also mean searching for alternative resources and technologies for replacement.

CHAPTER TWO

A BACKGROUND PROBE OF CONFLICTS IN THE NIGER DELTA REGIONS

The Niger Delta region is located in the Southern part of Nigeria which is made up of nine states comprising: Abia, Akwa Ibom, Bayelsa, Cross River, Delta, Edo, Imo, Ondo and Rivers States. The region is rich with abundant natural resources which accounts for more than 95 percent of Nigeria's earnings from export and more than 83 percent of the nation's revenue and the GDP is estimated to be approximately 40 percent[3]. The region has experienced various degrees of violence and conflicts for many years after crude oil was first discovered in Oloibiri, a community in Bayelsa State. Most of the areas in the region are made up of creek and water which makes it difficult for the building and establishment of settlements in the area.

The estimated population of the region is about 32million people with over 40 ethnic groups speaking more than 120 different languages as shown in *Table 1.1* below. The main occupations of the people are fishing and farming, especially in the rural areas. According to an NNDC report of 2005, the informal sector in the

---

[3] Onimode,2001, Onosode,2003; Imobigbe,2004

urban areas is involved in trading which comprises twenty percent of the total employment while services comprise 9 percent. Youths from the rural areas most times are not always interested in farming, as such, they mostly migrate to urban areas in search of better job opportunities and livelihood.

According to research, a high percentage of people living in the Niger Delta did not perform very well when compared to people from other regions of the country on various social indicators such as health, education, safety and security and in terms of a clean and a healthy environment.

From the indices, the Niger Delta region has one of the highest levels of infant mortality rate in Nigeria (35% - 48% per 1,000 according to NDHS reports of 1999) when measured according to general welfare with other regions. One amazing discovery was that, despite the huge oil revenue that accrues to the Federal Government from the region, it still has a high rate of unemployment and underemployment accounting to more than 80 percent among the youth population in Nigeria[4]. This situation contributed, largely to the violent conflict and youth restiveness in the region. The violent conflict that has ravaged the region for decades has threatened the security of the lives and properties of the people in the region and the economic stability of the country.

The Niger Delta region experienced the first violent militancy in February 1966. An Ijaw activist and community crusader named Isaach Boro from Oloibiri formed the Niger Delta Volunteer Force. He declared independence of the region from Nigeria and called it the Niger Delta People's Republic. It was made up of the present-day Delta, Rivers and Bayelsa States. The agitation and revolt of Isaac Boro initiated the civil war of 1967 known as the Biafra Civil War and the main cause and motivation of the agitation and conflicts was

---

4 National Bureauof Statistics,2005

mainly the control of revenue from oil proceeds. As a self-acclaimed leader of the Niger Delta People's Republic, Isaach Boro demanded that multinationals and oil companies operating in the region should negotiate directly with his self-acclaimed government rather than the Nigerian Government. The Eastern region at that time took the same step with the declaration of the Biafra State which eventually led to the civil war in 1967. The hope of the agitators for the resource control was frustrated when the Federal Government, through its legislatures, legitimised its sole control of the resources by the Petroleum Decree of 1969 which gave the Federal Government the sole right, control and ownership of every natural and mineral resource in the country. This was followed by the Land Use Act of 1978 which also gave the Federal Government the right to be the sole owner of all lands in the country's production. The ownership and control of the resources of the region by the Federal Government became so strong that it led to the aggravation of tension between the central government and the minority groups in the region because the region felt that they were grossly marginalised from the economic and political system by the majority groups that were represented in the Central Government. Apart from the marginalisation of the Niger Delta region from the economic and political system of the state, the continuous and persistent degradation and pollution of the environment as a result of oil exploration, exploitation and impoverishment by multinationals and oil companies operating in the region, also increased the anger and frustration of the people against the Federal Government.

In 2009, the Nigerian Military carried out an onslaught against the various militant groups in the Niger Delta which were significantly defeated through an aerial bombardment of their hideouts in the forests. This event significantly brought a level of peace in the region due to the fact that after the militants were defeated, the Nigerian Government, led by the late President Musa Yar'Adua granted amnesty to all militant groups with the condition that they should submit all their remaining weapons[5].

In the course of two years, more than 25,000 ex-militants (including women) accepted the amnesty and were engaged in different processes of the Amnesty Programme which was aimed at the disarmament, demobilisation, reorientation and reintegration of the militants into the society to live a normal and meaningful life in the society. In 2011, the estimated cost of the Amnesty Programme cost the Nigerian Government a whopping sum of $660 million[6]. Each of the ex-militants received N65,000 ($433) as monthly stipends which was more than thrice the minimum wage at that time. Sometimes, this money was unevenly distributed and at other times they were just misappropriated and embezzled by the commandants of the various ex-militant groups.[7]

The administration of the then president was praised and celebrated by stakeholders for introducing such programmes that brought relative peace to the troubled and conflicted region. This also brought a rise in the national income of the country via oil export because multinational oil companies were able to carry out their business operations without any form of disruption to their operations as was often the case before the Amnesty Programme.

The management of the Amnesty Programme was directly under the Office of the President because it was considered to be one of the pressing issues that had not only affected the level of oil production and exportation, lives and property of the people in the region, operations of multinational companies operating in the region but also the international image of the country. As such, the government thought that it would be more effective and the objective of the

---

[5] Folarinmi 2011
[6] Akintola 2011
[7] Akintola 2011

Amnesty Programme could be realised in the shortest possible time if the management of the programme was placed under the supervision of the Office of the Presidency. This decision of putting the programme under the supervision of the President also gave the ex-militants some level of confidence and trust in the programme due to the fact that the Vice President at that time, Goodluck Ebele Jonathan, who later became the President after the death of President Musa Yar'Adua is also a son from the Niger Delta region. Thus, relative peace returned to the region because of the political and financial influence from the presidency.

The Amnesty Programme was applauded by both local and international stakeholders but as common in most programmes, there were a lot of challenges that were encountered in the programme. Some ex-militant leaders abused the process by making unnecessary demands from the government for contracts and political favours, demands which were not part of the terms of the Amnesty Programme. They even sometimes, threatened the government that if their demands were not met, they would return to the creeks and resume violent conflict in the region. Other ex-militant groups also demanded an increase in their pay as against the actual amount they agreed to be paid prior to the Amnesty Programme. These and many more were the challenges that the Office of the President encountered during the Amnesty Programme. There was also a growing fear and concern that the ex-militants might return to start the conflict at the end of the Amnesty Programme which was slated to come to an end in 2015 which, coincidentally, was an election year in Nigeria. Stakeholders were really disturbed about what may happen in the region when the Amnesty Programme officially came to an end.

On the other hand, the Nigerian Military wanted the government to introduce a tougher and stricter policy to be able to achieve the aim of the Amnesty Programme which was primarily the disarmament and complete surrender of all the weapons that were still in the possession of the ex-militants because it was widely believed that the ex-militants did not submit all the weapons that they had during the disarmament exercise. This was a cause for concern to the Nigeria Military because they thought that if the ex-militants still had some weapons in their arsenal, they were more likely to go back to the creeks and start the violence in the region again when the Amnesty Programme came to an end. 2015 was considered a challenging year for the country because it was an election year.

Two main aims of the Amnesty Programme included restoring peace to the region, re-orientating and reintegrating all the ex-militants back into the society so that they could live meaningful lives and become responsible members of the society. By July 2011, almost 19,567 ex-militants, including women, had successfully scaled through the mandatory two-weeks course on non-violence. Also, 3,221 took part in various training and skill acquisition programmes of their choice and interest at various Nigerian training institutions. In addition, another 1,019 went through specialised training on specialised disciplines like Under-water Wielding, Aeronautical Engineering, Marine Engineering, Boat Building etc. in different countries such as the U.S, India, Malaysia, South Africa, Sri Lanka, Russia, Belarus and Poland[8].

The Nigerian Government also established what was called the Amnesty Projects. These projects were meant to create job opportunities for the ex-militants when they finished their trainings so that they could contribute meaningfully to the economic development of the country. The government also liaised with stakeholders, both private and public, to assist with technical and financial support, training and logistics, especially in the area of employment opportunities, in order to achieve the reintegration part of the Amnesty Programmes where the ex-militants would be

---

[8] Ujah2011;Ehigiator,2011

fully reintegrated into the society. Oil companies that operated in the region made a pledge to the government to give job placements to 3000 ex-militants when they completed their training and to also give various contracts like securing the coast and areas where they have their pipeline and installations to a number of ex-leaders of the various militant groups.

Table 1: The Niger Delta at a Glance

Sector	Information
States that are in the South-South zone Extended states that make up the Niger Delta region	Akwa Ibom, Bayelsa, Cross River, Delta, Edo, Rivers Abia, Imo and Ondo.
Population	32 million (22% of total Nigerian population) 60% of the population is under 30 years of age.
Ethnic Groups/Languages	40 main ethnic groups, around 120 mutually unintelligible languages and dialects
Land Area	112,000km of the land is affected by oil, primarily. Delta is 750,000kmsq.
Ecological Zone	Freshwater swamp, mangrove swamp, coast area sand ridges, lowland and forest
Energy	Generating energy through the burning of firewood is the main source of energy. 73% of the people make use of this source of energy while 34% have access to electric power.
Livelihood	Agriculture and fishing are the primary occupation of the people in the region which accounts for 48% of the people's source of living.
Water	50-55% of those in the urban area and 76%-80% in the rural area don't have access to safe and drinkable water.
Natural resources	Arable Land, Lead, Natural Gas, Tin, Petroleum and Zinc

Poverty	43% are relatively poor, while 57% consider themselves as poor.
Infant mortality rate	120 per a thousand (Nigeria: 100 per thousand)

Table 2: Unemployment and Underemployment Rate of 2016 (Youth)

State	Unemployment	Underemployment
Akwa Ibom	11.3(33)	33.7(24)
Bayelsa	6.8 (19)	19.4 (16)
Cross River	1.8(5)	12.0(9)
Delta	9.3(21)	29.2(27)
Edo	8.0(2.2)	30.9(37)
Rivers	11.4(29)	25.3(20)
South-South	8.8(24)	26.3(22)
Nigeria	5.3(14)	20.2(17.2)

Source: Nigeria Core Welfare Indicators Questionnaire 2006

Source: Niger Delta Partner Initiative (NDPI)

17

THE CAUSE OF THE CONFLICT IN THE NIGER DELTA

Natural resources refer to any material within the natural environment that can be harnessed for the utmost good and benefit of man[9]. Unfortunately, oil, which is the main source of income to Nigeria since it was discovered and explored in Oloibiri in Bayelsa State in 1956, has consistently been a source of deep-seated acrimony, contradiction and violent conflict in the Niger Delta region. The contention for resource control in the region has a long history.

During the 18th and 19th centuries, the struggle to participate actively in trade, especially palm oil, and self- succession by the Niger Delta community was a critical issue at the time. The tendency toward self-assertion and the desire not to be dominated by any foreign group or government was evident and illustrated by the resistance put up by King Williams Koko of Nember, Nana Olomu of Itsekiriland and King Jaja of Opobo. It was argued that the agitation and struggle for participation and control of the palm oil trade eventually became one of the development factors which include the Indirect Rule concept that was introduced by the British, military conquest and the revocation of the Royal Dutch Company as well as Christianity and the introduction of Western education[10]. All these gave rise to a new traditional elite.

During the pre-independence era, the fear and agitation for control were exemplified by the ethnic minorities, particularly in the Niger Delta, as the fear of domination was exemplified by the majority ethnic groups. These majority groups demanded the creation of more states and their agitations led to the formation of numerous political parties such as the Benin and Delta People's Party formed

---

[9] Faniran&Ojo,1981
[10] Douglas (2001:1)

in 1953, Midwest State Movement (1956), Calabar-Ogoja-Rivers State Movement (1954), United Middle Belt Congress, the Borno Youth Movement among others.[11] It is important to note that although the ethnic minorities cited their concern for an effective federal structure as a justification for more states but their main reason for the agitation was the need to have a direct control over the revenue accruable from the resources within their domain which would make it possible within the context of their own state. In 1990, the Movement for the Survival of the Ogoni People (MOSOP) led by its founder and activist Ken Saro-Wiwa sought a bill titled ***The Rights of the Ogoni People,*** that demanded the control of the resources in their domain and self-determination for the Ogoni people. Also, the Ogbia Charter demanded self-determination for the people of Ogbia in the Niger Delta region.

However, the Kaiama Declaration of 11th December 1998 represents the strongest and sharpest articulation and presentation for the demand for resource control. A study[12] opines that through the declaration, the Ijaw people proclaimed and made a strong demand for resource control and therefore prepared the ground for the current debate on the issue. The declaration of the Kaiama people has been followed by many proclamations, bills of rights, resolutions and charters of demands from many ethnic nationalities in the Niger Delta region such as the Urhobo, Ibibio, Itsekiri, Oron, Egi and Ikwere. Generally, the demand for self-determination and agitation for resource control can be classified into two broad phases which are:

i. The period of peaceful demonstration and demand for self-determination

---

[11] Ali (2003:78)
[12] Douglas(2001:2)

ii.   The beginning of armed struggle and demand for resource control.

Many economists and social scientists argue that there are two main issues that form the basis of the struggle by the people in the Niger Delta region. The first is the demand for self-determination. A study[13] emphasized that self-determination is the choice of a group of people defined by their territorial borders to live together in their own way, decide to run their own political system, promote, preserve and develop their own affairs as they choose, for the interest of its people. Self-determination refers to the expression of freedom by a group of people who consider themselves to be oppressed, subordinated, marginalised and dominated by the ruling class to constitute and establish themselves into an independent state. The right and freedom of individuals or groups of people that seek freedom and liberation from any form of oppression, deprivation and marginalisation on the basis of religion, culture, economics and politics is enshrined and guaranteed in the African Charter of Human Rights and the United Nations Declaration of Human Rights of 1948.

Self-determination refers to a situation where a group of people choose and decide to exist independently to manage and develop their social, political and economic affairs and to maintain full control and sovereignty of their resources. From the above expression, self- determination does not completely mean that the group of people want to exist separately and completely on their own. Rather, they want to have an autonomy of their social, political and economic affairs. They want to decide their affairs in every sense rather than being controlled, subordinated and marginalised by the Central Government. Over the years, all over the world, the right of freedom to self-determination by people has given rise to

_____

13 Okwu-Okafor(1994:89)

nationalism and various movements that organise protests which, at times, give rise to conflict, violence and the breakdown of law and order in the society.

The recent calls for self-determination were from the Scottish people who clamoured for independence from the United Kingdom. They went into a referendum but unfortunately for them, those who wanted Scotland to remain under the United Kingdom were more than those who clamoured for an independent Scotland. Their demands and protests were peaceful and non-violent. Self-determination, in the simplest form, refers to a demand for a socio-political and economic autonomy and the full control and sovereignty of their resources by a certain group of people.

Several times, the agitation for self-determination has degenerated to violent conflict and even escalated to civil war, especially in Africa. The rise of self-determination in Nigeria, particularly in the Niger Delta region, was due to the marginalisation of the minorities, deprivation, exploitation, pollution and degradation of the environment which significantly affected the livelihood of the people in the region since most of their means of livelihood are farming and fishing, lack of political representation in the Central Government and lack of a sustainable development plan for the region by the Central Government even though the region contributes more than 80% of the country's export and more than 70% of the national earnings.

The second basis of the struggle of the Niger Delta people is the struggle for resource control. The groups that clamour for resource control believe that when the region is in full control of their resources they will be able to achieve some significant level of development because they know better and understand the terrain and know the challenges that the region is facing, in terms of their priority need and what needs urgent attention. They argue that the Central Government is insensitive to the plights and challenges of the people in the region and lacks the political will to show any sustainable development plans it has for the region. They are of the view that the demand for resource control will be the beginning of a new phase of developmental strides in the region. They argue that the demand, struggle and agitation for resource control is non-negotiable because resource control is an essential and fundamental component of the survival and existence of the Niger Delta people.

One of the important documents where the concept of resource control is well articulated is the document referred to as the Kaiama Declaration. The Kaiama Declaration was the declaration made by the Ijaw people on 11th December 1998. The term "resource control" was well articulated and popularised in article 1, 2 and 4 of the document, and it gave rise to various debates in recent times by policy makers, social scientists and stakeholders in the region. Article 1 of the declaration states that, *"the ownership of all land and natural resources within the territory of the Ijaw people belongs to the Ijaw communities because they are **'the basis of their survival'"***

Article 2 emphasises the "people's and communities' full right of ownership and control of their lives and resources", while Article 4 states that "all multinationals and oil companies and their personnel operating in Ijaw land and communities should leave "pending when the issue of resource ownership and control in the Ijaw domain is fully resolved'".

The multinational oil companies operating in the region and the Nigerian Government have a different view and as such, they do not agree with the various terms in the articles concerning the concept of resource control as enshrined in the Kaiamaa Declaration. On the part of the multinational oil companies, they have a different view of resource control. They think that the agitation and struggle for resources by the youths in the Niger Delta region is a clamour that part of the proceeds and revenue that accrue from the export and sale of crude oil should be invested into the region for the economic growth and development of the region. They see it that the clamour for resource control is a fiscal federalism exercise by the people, not necessarily a complete change of ownership and control of the resources as stated in the Kaiama Declaration because they believe when they settle Nigeria in the form of taxes and royalties, they will not have any problem in the host communities in which they do business. After all, it is the government's responsibility to provide security and the enabling environment to do business. So, they expect peace in carrying out their business operations.

On the part of the Nigerian Government, they see the agitation, struggle and advocacy for resource control as not only a call for the breakdown of law and order in the region, but also a call for the breakup of the country. The Nigerian State believes that the advocacy and agitation for resource control is a call for secession by separatists and they are not ready to tolerate any form of secession tendencies whatsoever and to such, they are willing and ready to stop such an attempt with any available means at their disposal.

From the analysis above, the agitation and struggle for resource control has been a struggle that was aimed at putting an end to the many years of marginalisation, subjection, exclusion, oppression, domination, exploitation and injustice meted out on the people of the Niger Delta region by multinational oil companies and the Nigerian Government.

The Niger Delta people claimed that their struggle and advocacy for resource control and self-determination was due to the continuous denial and violation of their fundamental human rights by the Nigerian Government. The struggle by the youth in the region necessitated the establishment of the resistance movement with the aim of realising their self-determination agenda which they believe is the only means to achieve their social, political and economic autonomy from the Nigerian State. The establishment of the movements was a direct expression that was taken by the various ethnic nationalities in the region to make known their demands through the issuing of the bill of rights for the demand of their freedom, access to their basic needs and resources, the protection of their means of livelihood from environmental pollution and degradation and for inclusion and equal participation in the political sphere of the country.

THE ROLE OF POVERTY IN THE NIGER DELTA CONFLICT

In analysing the cause of violent conflict in the Niger Delta region, many economists and political scientists have argued that there is a significant relationship between violent conflict in a region and poverty. There are several arguments that link the violent conflict in the Niger Delta to extreme poverty in the region, apart from the various factors stated above.

According to the World Bank definition of poverty, anyone who lives below a dollar a day is considered to be poor. On the other hand, poverty can be defined as a situation where people cannot afford their basic needs for a decent livelihood. It deprives people of making basic choices and having opportunities for their total wellbeing. Since poor people have no means of making choices for a decent and meaningful life, according to Maslow's Theory in the quest for survival, they may resort to violence at some point, if such can give them their desired level of need and comfort.

All over the world, especially in countries that are poor, poverty has been said to be the main reason and trigger of conflicts. Many analysts argue that meaningful development cannot be attained in the societal and economic system of a state if the state undermines practical links between poverty and conflict. In more practical terms, conflict increases poverty, decreases economic growth, prevents investors from investing in the region and undermines the developmental structure on which a society can attain economic growth and progress.

According to HDR 2005, conflict is the opposite of human development. In this chapter, I argued that among other causes of conflicts, poverty is a factor that triggers and aggravates conflict in the region that is blessed with natural resources yet, its inhabitants are known to be among the poorest and most wretched in the country due to persistent violence that has undermined the economic development in the region.

In recent times, the concept of poverty has been broadening through the work of many scholars and economists. According to the Research Council of Norway[14], "People are considered poor if they lack the freedom and ability to meet daily needs for themselves and their dependents". One of the broad explanations of poverty is the lack of human capacity to obtain minimum living conditions, the lack of access to welfare and also the lack of meaningful resources that can enable people to improve their well-being and living conditions. In the broader definition of poverty, it has gone beyond just economics; it also includes cultural, political and social issues that undermine the well-being of people. A study[15] opines that when people are unable to meet certain basic human needs, it can lead to a reaction that can escalate to violent conflict. Furthermore, when people are denied, not only their biological need, but also their psychological needs that could promote growth and development, it can generate conflict in the society.

The various causes of conflict are the focus in this chapter and that the importance of basic needs like food, shelter, water, functional educational and health care systems cannot be overemphasised or ignored. It is also to be noted that anything that tries to undermine

---

[14] Research Council of Norway (2005:4)
[15] Burton(1997)

these basic needs can generate conflicts. Aristotle asserted that it is not the nature of humans to be involved in social strife, revolt or revolution, rather, humans involve in social strife and revolution due to poverty and uneven distribution of resources by the ruling class. A society that is poor and is deprived of their basic needs amidst abundant resources that are in their domain will be forced to revolt to seek justice through any means whatsoever, including violence, if they think that by it, they can achieve their goals.

THE EFFECTS OF CONFLICT ON THE OIL-PRODUCING COMMUNITIES

The effects suffered and the costs continually incurred by conflicts on the oil-producing communities in the Niger Delta states are enormous and the loss they have suffered due to oil exploitation and spillage are immeasurable when compared to the supposed gains that the multinationals are claiming to have contributed to the host community. The negative impact of oil production has severely affected the traditional livelihood of the people and have created a propensity for conflict and violence. The Niger Delta region has experienced both violent intra and inter communal conflicts and clashes with oil companies in which the critical and challenging issues involved have not been resolved. Notable conflicts that are linked and related to oil exploitation in the Niger Delta region are the conflicts between the Ijaw in Nembe/Kalabari, Basambiri/Ogbomari and Okpoma/Brass in Bayelsa Sate. Also, in Ondo State, there were conflicts between the Ilaje/ Ijaw. There was also an inter-ethnic conflict that happened between the Ogoni/Adoni and Ogoni/Okrika in Rivers State.[16]

---

[16] Human Rights Watch, 1999, 2002, 2005; Environmental Rights Action 2000; Imobighe 2004;

The primary causes of these conflicts were clashes of ownership of land where oil wells were located and claims to oil company compensations and contracts. The loss of many lives and destruction of properties due to violent inter-communal and inter-ethnic conflict is by far more than the conflict within the community or ethnic group and between the community and the oil companies or government. The constant conflicts in the oil-producing areas affected the people adversely, particularly the women and children who have been internally displaced. The psychosocial impact on them is enormous.[17] The consequences of the violent conflict may range from disruption of children's education due to insecurity and displacement and the inability to cater for the children as a result of disruption of economic activities, to exposure, trauma and diseases. It was revealed in this study[18] that the internal displacement caused by the violent conflict has resulted in the loss of livelihood in the form of physical, financial, human, social and economic assets.

The response of the State's management to the conflict has taken an enormous toll on the region, in terms of loss of lives and property, livelihood, as well as physical infrastructures. The state security agencies have been accused of recklessness, ruthlessness, brutality and the use of excessive force in resolving the conflicts. The state security agents have also been known to attack and indiscriminately shoot in towns and villages, burn property and raze communities. They also kill, torture, flog and rape civilians and protesters.[19]

People in the communities have been forced to flee, thereby creating and swelling internal displacement. For a long time, oil companies hid behind the shield of security agencies to institute a regime of corporate responsibility and sensitivity to host communities. A published study argues that it is alleged that some

---

[17] Obi,1998
[18] Ukeje(2001) and Ojo(2002)
[19] Human Rights Watch1999

of the oil companies purchase arms, as well as provide logistics and support for state security in their repression and brutality against community members. Although, it is difficult to verify the allegations that the oil companies provided ammunition for the security agents, it has been argued that their practices generated resistance by the inhabitants of the region and finally produced a ragtag army of enraged, lawless and militant youths.[20]

Violent and accidental deaths have also been caused by tampering with oil pipelines and illegal bunkering by some members of the host communities who have no knowledge of the risk and hazard associated with tampering with the oil pipelines as an unauthorised person. Such places where the oil facilities are located are highly risky and unauthorized persons are highly prohibited from gaining entrance to such sites and locations. Thousands lose their lives from pipeline explosions that eventually occur when they try to steal crude oil. Another dimension of the environmental cost of the oil activities which happened often between 1993 and 2001 is related to fire and explosion due to the vandalisation of crude oil facilities by youths in the oil-producing communities. A particular example is the leakage fire explosion that occurred in October 1998 in Jesse community in Delta State which killed more than 700 people, many of whom were women and children.[21] Similarly, in early May 2006, another fire explosion incident occurred when a pipeline exploded outside the commercial capital city of Lagos[22]. The fire explosions in Oko, Ebute, Ijala Swamp, Oviri Court, Jesse and other parts of the country have wreaked a severe havoc of destruction on human lives and on the environment through the loss of several hectares of farmlands and plantations.

---

[20] Onojowo,2001
[21] TheGuardian7November1998
[22] InternationalCrisisGroup,2006

Oil pipeline vandalisation took a dramatic turn in the mid-1990s. There were 524 cases of pipeline rupture recorded in 1999 of which 497 were related to vandalisation. By the end of 2000, the cases of vandalisation of oil pipelines in the Niger Delta reached almost 800. Thousands have perished from these spillages and leakages, which often occur as a result of the sabotage of oil pipelines. The economic cost of these acts of vandalisation has been enormous at both local and national levels. This is often linked to the shortage of petroleum products and black *marketeering*, the sales of adulterated fuel, and lower refinery utilisation due to disruption of crude oil supply to the Kaduna Refinery. These harmful behavioural patterns generally reflect the economic, political and environmental discontent in the region[23].

Due to the consistent sabotage of the oil facilities of the multinational companies, they, in turn, resort to the use of mobile police forces as security to guard their facilities and installations. This gave rise to the abuse of human rights by the security forces employed by the multinational companies, particularly Shell. The Umuechem incident of 1990 in which Shell used these security forces, led to the killing of 80 unarmed civilians and the destruction of homes[24]. Because of the murder of the policemen that were sent to investigate the activities of youth militants in Odi Community in Bayelsa State, the Armed Forces attacked Odi Communities in reprisal and this led to the death of 100 inhabitants, the displacement of thousands of people and a countless number of destroyed houses and properties. Graffiti was found that included ethnic slurs and reflected views that the town and the whole Ijaw ethnic group be punished for the crimes committed by their youth[25].

---

[23] Ikporukpo,1996; Iwayemi,2006
[24] HumanRight Watch 1999
[25] HumanRightWatch,2002;Albert,2003

The protest by the oil-producing communities against the multinational companies for the environmental degradation caused by the oil exploitation in their communities were met with brutal force by both the oil companies and the government. A particular incident occurred in May 1998 when youths in Ilaje Community in Ondo's State staged a peaceful protest at the Chevron Parable Platform off Awoye Coast, demanding running water, greater local employment, medical facilities and the fulfilment of pledges made by Chevron to grant scholarships to local students. Their protest was met with brutal forces attached to guard Chevron facilities, resulting in the death of two youths and a host of others injured[26]. Similarly, in 1996, the protest by the Movement for the Survival of the Ogoni People (MOSOP) which generated international attention, ultimately led to the hanging of Ken Saro-Wiwa and eight other members of MOSOP. The government, which at that time was led by Late Gen. Sani Abacha, responded by creating a special security force, The Rivers State Internal Security Task Force which was responsible for the death of hundreds of the Ogonis during the period it occupied Ogoniland from 1993-1998[27]. It is difficult and complex to conclude that the cost to the host communities of violent conflict in the Niger Delta region is enormous and of greater magnitude than the benefit that they derived from the oil exploitation since oil was first discovered in Oloibiri, in Bayelsa State, Nigeria, in 1956.

---

[26] EnvironmentalRightsAction,1999;HumanRightsWatch;1999
[27] HumanRightWatch,2002

PEACEFUL DEMONSTRATION AND ADVOCACY FOR SELF-DETERMINATION

In 1957, the minorities presented testimonies before the Willink Commission of Enquiry about their problems and fears concerning the situation before the emergence of the Nigerian state. It was argued that during that period, many protests and demands for equity, justice and fairness in the scheme of things were registered and made known to the authorities without achieving any positive result[28]. The people from the oil-producing areas resorted to seeking redress in the court of law but their litigation usually ended in unfavourable verdicts. The people did not relent and they embarked on other peaceful and legal means to express their griefs and why it was necessary for them to control the resources within their domain. Correspondence was sent to the colonial government then and also to the post-independent Nigeria administration on the challenges and problems of the Niger Delta region. Due to the consistent failure of this approach and all other peaceful means, the people decided to seek redress and make their position known. The agitators made further moves by electing representatives that would liaise with the government at all levels to make their demands known and to achieve the desired results. A study[29] asserts that most often, no meaningful achievement and success on their demand was recorded. It was just warm receptions and empty promises they always got from the authorities. During this period, demonstrations were staged also in the Niger Delta region and other places where pamphlets and banners were printed and displayed to further draw attention to the consistent conflicts in the Niger Delta region. Correspondence was sent to various affected state capitals, Lagos and Abuja in order to inspire and get the attention of the

---

[28] Jimoh (2008)
[29] (Saliu, 2008)

31

government. Nevertheless, things remained the same and nothing really changed. On the other hand, the demand for externalisation and self-determination by the Niger Delta people began evolving because of the consistent increase in the ownership, control and management of the oil resources by the central government and the distribution of the revenue to the disadvantage and detriment of the oil-producing states.

Asobi[30] puts it this way:

> *"In seeking to fund the war and sourcing money for running the economy, the Federal Government (still dominated by the transformed Northern and Western faction of the ruling class) legislated via decrees, the collection and sharing of oil revenue to itself. Since Nigeria came to rely totally on oil revenue the hegemonic faction of the majority nationalities now had control over the fiscal basis of the state, to the exclusion of the oil minorities".*

This was as against the principle of the Fiscal Federal Decree 51 of 1969 that vested power on the central government to the sole and complete ownership, control and management of all petroleum and mineral resources in Nigeria. Also, the Offshore Oil Revenue Decree Number 9 gave the central government total control of the entire revenue that accrues from the sales of offshore oil and increases the dependence of the minority on the majority in the sharing of their own oil resources. As such, the minority ethnic nationalities that hosts the oil resources were deprived the right, control and benefits of their resources and this triggered and aggravated the agitation between them and the Nigerian Government. The taking over of

---

[30] Asobi(2008)

control of the oil and stifling of the derivation principle by the Federal Government made the minority ethnic nationality who own the resources to oppose domination by the major nationalities and they devised new strategies with the objectives of externalising their claims and grievances against the Nigerian State. Agitation and activist movements like the MOSOP, the Ijaw Youth Congress (IYC), the Ethnic Minority Rights Organisation of Africa (EMIROAF) and the Shikoku developed a national and clear agenda and had a solid organisation at the popular level. These groups were able to push the Niger Delta issues to the front burner of global discussions by raising awareness about the environmental hazards caused by oil and mining companies and highlighted the lack of representation of the Niger Delta People.[31] The arrest and execution of Ken Saro-Wiwa with eight others of his Ogoni compatriots by the Abacha Government in 1995 drew public outrage and brought substantial international attention to the pathetic condition of the people[32].

THE BEGINNING OF ARMED STRUGGLE ERA IN THE NIGER DELTA REGION

The first significant use of arms in agitating for the plight of the Niger Delta region was in 1966 by Adaka Borro and there were no other agitations using arms again until the 1990s when the ethnic militias that violently protested against the economic and political marginalisation of the Niger Delta region by the Federal Government emerged[33]. There are two traceable events that give rise to the wave of violence in the region and Nigeria in general. The administrations of Gen. Babangida and Abacha did not allow or tolerate any form of

---

[31] Obi 2000:87-88
[32] Asuni. 2009: 1
[33] Asuni. 2009

agitation or protest and the Odi massacre in Bayelsa State occurred during the administration of the civilian President, Chief Olufemi Obasanjo. These two events contributed to the escalation of violent conflict and youth restiveness in the Niger Delta region. The character and operation of the regimes, particularly the Babangida and Abacha regimes, escalated and deepened the crises of the Nigerian State resulting in the continuous rise of various ethnic militias. The people in the Niger Delta region reacted by increasing the tempo of militancy and adopting armed struggle in their demand for justice from both the government and the oil companies.

It is important to say here that the ethnic militia is the extreme form of ethnic agitation for self-determination. In this case, the agitated group adopts a militant style and character of approach that develops into a full militant group with each having its own ethnic identity and agenda which is to act as a medium for the actualisation of its people's desires and aspirations. A study[34] opined that these ethnic movements have their ethnic identities and characteristics, such as the use of violence as a means to seek fundamental change in the status quo. Some of the common and prominent ethnic militia group in the Niger Delta include the Niger Delta Vigilante Group (NDVG), the Ijaw National Congress, Niger Delta People Volunteer Force, the Urhobo National Union, the Greenlanders and the Egbesu ethnic groups.

Although the origins of the Niger Delta armed groups in the various Niger Delta states vary from state to state there is a general belief that gives a conviction about the origin of these armed groups in the Niger Delta region. Recent studies have shown that most of these armed groups were established on university campuses and then found their way into street gangs, entered illegal activities like oil bunkering and illicit drug trafficking and from time to time,

---

[34] Agbu (2002)

especially during political elections, served as thugs to rig elections in favour of those who patronise them.

Due to the consistent rise of various armed groups, it is difficult to know the number of people that are involved in ethnic militancy in the Niger Delta, but recent studies and research show that there are at least, forty-eight groups in Delta State alone with over twenty-five thousand members, having a military arsenal of about ten thousand weapons. All the groups enjoy the tacit support of local communities in solidarity against the exploitation of their region by the oil companies, the states and the Federal Government. Furthermore, other groups depend on the patronage from politicians who use them to attack and intimidate their political opponents, while others are involved and engaged by military officers and politicians to prop their criminal activities such as arms importation and oil bunkering. It is also suggested that there are six thousand armed militants in the Niger Delta [35]. These figures show how serious and critical these problems are and the challenges that the states in the Niger Delta region and the Federal Government are facing in terms of disarmament, demobilisation and the final stage, which is integrating them back into the society to live a normal, productive and responsible life in the society, thereby contributing in a more meaningful way to the socio-economic development of their states, in particular, and Nigeria in general. As it has been said, before the ethnic militancy in the Niger Delta, the conflict in the region is usually caused by some critical issues and grievances against the government and oil multinational companies.

One of the primary issues making the oil-producing areas to agitate is that the Federal Government is consistently using and deploying a greater part of the huge revenue being generated from the oil-producing minorities to finance the infrastructural development of

---

[35] Asuni;(2009)

other states, towns and villages of the majority at the expense and disadvantage of the minorities that produce the crude oil. This one-sided developmental approach due to favouritism, tribalism and nepotism is visible by the huge federal funding of big projects like the funding of dam and irrigation projections and also the subsidising of agricultural and social development programmes in the region of the majority. [36]The locations of the state-owned socio-economic projects like the Kaduna Refinery, and the headquarters of many educational, administrative and military institutions are located in the areas of the major ethnic groups. However, the minorities continue to live in squalor, depravity and abject poverty irrespective of the abundant resources and oil wealth. Of all the oil-producing communities, the Ogoni Community in Rivers State is seen to be the luckiest and advantageous because of the huge amount it has contributed to the revenue generation of the Nigerian State. It is on record between 1958, the early stage of oil exploration and exploitation in Nigeria and 1992 that the Ogoni oil community has generated for Nigeria, a revenue of about 40 billion Dollars[37]. Furthermore, the Ogoni Community accrued revenue from oil for the government to the tune of 6 billion Dollars between 1999 and 2004.[38] Despite the huge revenue the Ogoni Community have contributed to the revenue-base of Nigeria, the community has few oil fields, a large petrochemical plant, several oil serving companies that are closely located, Nigeria's only major fertilizer plant and the fourth largest ocean port. [39]

The case of Urhobo land in Delta State is more pathetic and even worse. In forty-one years, the petroleum industry in Nigeria, Shell, Pan Ocean and the Nigeria National Petroleum Corporation (NNPC) have generated and gained up to 2.2 trillion Naira, an average of 56

---

[36] Ovwasa (1999.89)
[37] OgoniBillofRight,(1992)
[38] Guardian, (18 April 2006)
[39] Naanen, 1995:1

billion Naira yearly.[40] The annual budget of Delta State is 4 billion yet the state contributed at least 36% of the Gross Domestic Product (GDP) of the country. More alarming is that Urhoboland on a daily basis, loses about 68 million Naira worth of its natural gas as a result of gas flaring[41] with all this enormous contribution of Urhoboland via its oil wealth to the treasury of the Nigerian Government, Urhobo land does not have any significant and meaningful federal institution apart from the epileptic Warri Refinery and the inactive Aladja Steel complex that is going into extinction. It should be noted that before the establishment of the Federal University of Petroleum Resources in 2007/2008, Delta State did not have any Federal higher institution of learning for more than three decades except the Petroleum Training Institute (PTI) established to train skilled manpower for the oil and gas sector. However, there are federal institutions of higher learning or other form of federal institutions in almost all the majority states.[42] Another pressing issue that aggravated the bitterness of the Niger Delta people against the federal government was the degree of environmental degradation and pollution which resulted to the disruption of their major occupation and source of livelihood being farming and fishing. The socio-economic welfare and the health of the Niger Delta oil producing communities have suffered severe effects as a result of oil exploration and exploitation such as oil spillage into the lands, farmlands and swamps for many years. Oil exploration activities have often resulted in the destruction of the environment, erosion, destruction of aquatic life, extermination of some important soil organisms, promotion of malaria infestation due to the accumulation of water in the pits which serves as a breeding ground and lastly general ecological disturbances.[43]

---

[40] Ovwasa, (1998; 89).
[41] Guardian (19th, Aug 1998)
[42] Ovwasa (1998: 89)
[43] Jimoh, (2008: 11)

The tragic incident that occurred in Jesse community in Delta State where more than 1,200 people were burnt to death by petrol explosion occurred when they were trying to make a living from the leakage of petrol from a damaged pipe, shows the horrible situation that the oil communities are faced with on a daily basis in the struggle for survival.

Another contending issue that the people of the oil producing area in the Niger Delta region find very disturbing to handle is the political marginalisation that they have suffered for many years. This political marginalisation is evident in federal appointments in oil-related parastatals. They are not adequately represented in appointments into government offices and ministries especially. Ordinarily, under the federal character commission, preference ought to be given to indigenes of the oil communities in such appointments, but because of the political marginalisation, the principles upon which the Federal Character Commission was established has been utterly disregarded by the Federal Government by monopolising major appointments to the three major ethnic groups, with the Hausa-Fulani claiming the largest share[44].

The Agitation for resources control and revenue allocation by the poor and underdeveloped oil-producing communities in the Niger Delta region had now reached the extreme due to the grievances that have been accumulated for a very long time by the people in the oil producing communities. The Niger Delta People's Volunteer Force led by Alhaji Asari Dokubo in early 2004 threatened the unity of the state of Nigeria and promised a direct war against the oil companies operating in the region, states and Federal Government.[45]

---

[44] Ovwasa (1999: 89)
[45] Crisis Group Africa Report, (2006:6)

In September 2005, Asari Dokubo was arrested and detained by the government led by President Olusegun Obasanjo on the grounds of treason. This gave rise to other militant groups. To show their agitation, grief and continuous demand for the control of their oil wealth, compensation for the environmental pollution and degradation, and their demand for the release of Asari Dokubo, they launched an attack on oil installations in February 2006 causing a significant reduction of about 25% in Nigeria's oil output. They also kidnapped nine foreign oil workers but eventually released them in the following month of March, 2006 though threatened subsequent violence against the oil installations in the region. MEND executed its operations with high military sophistication and well-organised intelligence gathering which made it more advanced and tactical in mode of operation when compared to the other ethnic militant groups. Its threats of attack, most times, were delivered through email; one of these anticipated attacks pushed the price of crude oil to seventy dollars per barrel one year.

The large number of unemployed youths in the Niger Delta region, the availability of large number of firearms and the consistent conflict with the state and Federal Government have all combined to be a better recruitment platform for MEND and other militant groups to further increase their membership and further their militant demands and activities.

The agitation for resource control has taken a new dimension with women joining into the struggle when they started protesting against the severe injustices wrought against them by the multinational oil companies and the Federal Government. Women and children from the Ugborodo oil community in the year 2002 seized Chevron's Tanks, farms and terminal in Escravos. Also, women from the Gbaramutu Kingdom invaded NNPC/Chevron flow stations. Similarly, during the same period, the Itsekiri women in Warri under the auspices of Warri Women Consultative Assembly rose to speak on behalf of the Itsekiri people by threatening to seal off the oil wells in the Niger Delta. The involvement of women in militias' agitation in the Niger Delta is significant because they and their children are the greatest victims of the socio-economic and health effects of oil exploration and extraction[46].

AGITATION FOR RESOURCE CONTROL AND SUSTAINABLE DEVELOPMENT IN NIGERIA

Nigeria's development has been adversely affected in many ways by the crises caused by the persistent struggle, especially the violent agitation for the control of the oil wealth region by the various ethnic militant groups in the Niger Delta region. The violent confrontations constitute a serious danger to the safety of properties and individual's freedom in the Nigerian State. As said earlier, the activities of the various ethnic militant groups resulted in the great destruction of lives and properties, while the government's responses through military interventions and operations during crises has led to civilian casualty, killings and the destruction of the oil communities and these have brought severe consequences to the socio-economic systems of the people in the region. Although Nigeria had experienced some degree of violent conflict, youth restiveness and civil unrest in the past, the frequency and magnitude of violent activities since the beginning of this present democratic order starting from 1999 is indeed alarming and worrisome. Apart from engaging the state security forces in armed confrontation and shootings, the militants also engage in the killing, raiding, murdering and attempted murdering of political figures that they consider a threat to their operations. They are also involved in hostage taking which has become common in the region.

---

[46] Ugo (2004;68)

The magnitude of hostage taking has reached an alarming stage such that no one appears to be safe from their target. In bid to press their demand for the control of their own resources and the recognition of their ethnic nationalities in the Niger Delta, they currently take hostage, foreign and local workers of these oil multinational companies that operate on their soil, government officials and even their family members. The national economy has suffered adversely due to this violent agitation and struggle in the Niger Delta by these militants. This has become so obvious because the Nigerian economy is an oil-based economy that relies heavily on oil export for revenue generation; as such, whatever happens to the exploration, production and distribution of the oil community will definitely affect all other sectors of the economy. The violent conflict in the Niger Delta, the vandalisation of oil installation and bunkering has made the nation to record a huge loss in revenue generation. For example, in September 2009, the quantity of crude oil produced decreased by one million barrels daily due to the militant activities in the region. Such a decrease in the production of oil has consistently diminished the income of the government and the profit of oil companies. The rate of foreign investment has decreased due to the persistent violent agitation by the militants because an investor is very skeptical of the security situation of the country and would require a reasonable level of security to be able to invest and conduct businesses. Because of the violent agitation, conflicts and security challenges facing the country, many investors do not see Nigeria as an investor-friendly country. Another contending issue that the country is facing presently is the Boko haram insurgency which has put Nigeria's image in a bad light, thereby worsening the security situation and making it a no-go area for foreigners and foreign investors alike.

The security of the energy sector has also received a threat due to ethnic agitation for resource control, not only in Nigeria but also for the entire world. This is because some of the oil resources such as petroleum, gas and diesel are the basic source of power generation and supply to some industries and also for domestic consumption which is usually threatened and jeopardized when there is a wide spread of violence and criminal activities in areas where these resources are located. The Niger Delta's importance to global energy security was emphasised in a publication by the council on foreign relations:

> "Insecurity in the Niger Delta is a problem, and not only for the Nigerian government, it is also a problem for the United States and a problem to the international community. It is the United States' interest to improve its energy security and reduce the flow of arms, illicit oil, and illegal money transfer from Nigeria. A stable Niger Delta producing a steady supply of oil would also help to moderate world oil prices. It is therefore imperative that the United States and other international partners offer Nigeria all the help it needs to confront its armed groups. Because one thing is clear; allowing the problem to fester will be a recipe for further violence, instability and energy insecurity" (Asuni)

Similarly, the increasingly violent conflict in the Niger Delta region has affected the foreign policy of Nigeria in some ways. The image of the country has been greatly affected due to the persistent violent conflict in the Niger Delta region which has been widely publicised by the international media, thereby putting the image of the country in a bad light in the international community. It is common knowledge in this contemporary world, the international image of a country is very important if it must achieve the objectives of its foreign policies. Generally, many countries' view of Nigeria is that the country is not a safe place which makes foreign governments sometimes discourage their citizens from travelling to Nigeria. If they must travel to Nigeria, they must by all means, avoid going to the Niger Delta region.[47]

Also, the issue of hostage-taking in the region has really increased the fear of foreign citizens who are interested in coming to the country for either business purposes or for leisure and has continued to magnified Nigeria's level of corruption into a global level due to the huge sum of money that captives often pay to secure their release when they are kidnapped and taken hostage. It is believed that the huge ransom paid to the militants for the release of their captives always go to the unaudited accounts of the militants such that it makes it impossible for the money to be traced after the ransom has been paid. Also, the sovereignty of Nigeria is always compromised in recent times because foreign interests negotiate directly with militants for the release of their citizens when they are taken hostage without consulting and collaborating with the Nigerian Government and this undermines the sovereignty of Nigeria.

Moreover, the foreign policy of the country has suffered some setbacks due to the crises in the Niger Delta because these crises have undermined the laudable peace-keeping roles the country has been constantly playing across the world especially in West and Sub-Saharan Africa. Many people wonder in some quarters, how Nigeria cannot solve and manage her little problems in the Niger Delta region, yet she keeps exporting conflict resolution and peacekeeping mechanisms abroad.[48]

The violent agitation for the control of resources by the militants in the region has posed a greater threat to the nation's unity, stability and security. The escalating violent and consistent attacks on the country's assets by various militant groups pose a serious threat to

---

[47] Saliu,(2008:351)
[48] Saliu, (2008: 353)

the nation's nascent democracy, unity, stability and security. As one civil society leader noted, "the commitment to true federalism and democracy holds Nigeria together, and the lack of federalism and democracy threaten to tear Nigeria apart[49].

Another issue that should be a concern for national security is the source of the acquisition of weapons by the militants. Because of the sophistication of the weapons that are often used by the militants, there is a reason to believe that some of these weapons come from government armouries while others seem to enter the country through the porous borders.[50] Without any doubt, it is a known fact that the increasing violence in the Delta region undermines the integrity of Nigeria as a nation and presents the danger of possible attempts of coups and other desperate actions by those who feel that their privileges are being jeopardised.

WORLD NATURAL RESOURCES, MILITARY EXPENDITURE AND ECONOMIC GROWTH.

Since the year 2000, world military spending has increased rapidly to an estimated amount of $153.1 billion. The increase is 5.9 percent in real terms when compared with the military spending in the world as at 2008, which is 49 percent higher when compared with year 2000. The increase approximately represents 2.7 percent of the world's Gross Domestic Product (GDP), which is approximately $224 per person. The rapid rise in the military burden of the world's GDP in 2008 from 2.4 percent was as a result of an increase in the world's military spending, the increases in the value of the US dollar

---

[49] CrisisGroupAfricaReport, 2006: 1
[50] Asamu (2006: 131)

which increased the effect and impact of the high US military burden on the world scale and the fall in global GDP.

Many researchers opined that one of the factors that triggers the rise in military expenditure for the past decades is the rise in demand and prices of natural resources, most significantly oil. In Africa for example, the military expenditure in 2009 was estimated to have been $27.4 billion. When compared in real terms in 2008, there was a significant increase of 6.5 percent. Countries like Nigeria, Angola, Libya, Sudan and Chad have increased their military expenditure in the past decades due to a rapid rise in oil revenues, continuous military modernisation to meet up with the global security challenges such as terrorism as in the case of the Northern Part of Nigeria in the Boko Haram case, external invasion as in the case of Russia and Ukraine, internal security challenges as in the case of Libya and Sudan, civil unrest and violent conflict as witnessed in the Niger Delta region and economic growth. Economists and researchers have written extensively to confirm there is a significant link between natural resources and violent conflict onset[51]. In their works, they argue that the extraction of natural resources can generate civil conflict and also create the need for a government agency or institution to protect the resource infrastructure from any form of internal and external attack or threat. The inflow of oil revenue in poor African countries is more likely to increase the *"oil curse phenomenon"* which usually leads to the breakdown of law and order, civil conflict and lack of democratic dividends[52]. Currently, there are many works that are being done by researchers of Economics and Political Science to determine the role of natural resources especially oil as a determinant of military expenditure.

---

[51] Lujala (2010), Ross (2006), Humphrey (2005), Lujala et al (2005), Fearon (2005), CollierandHeoffler (2004) and Fearon and Laitin (2003)
[52] Ross (2012)

Figure 1. Shows the continuous increase in world and regional expenditure estimate from 2000 – 2009. The figures are in US$ at a constant 2008 price and exchange rate.

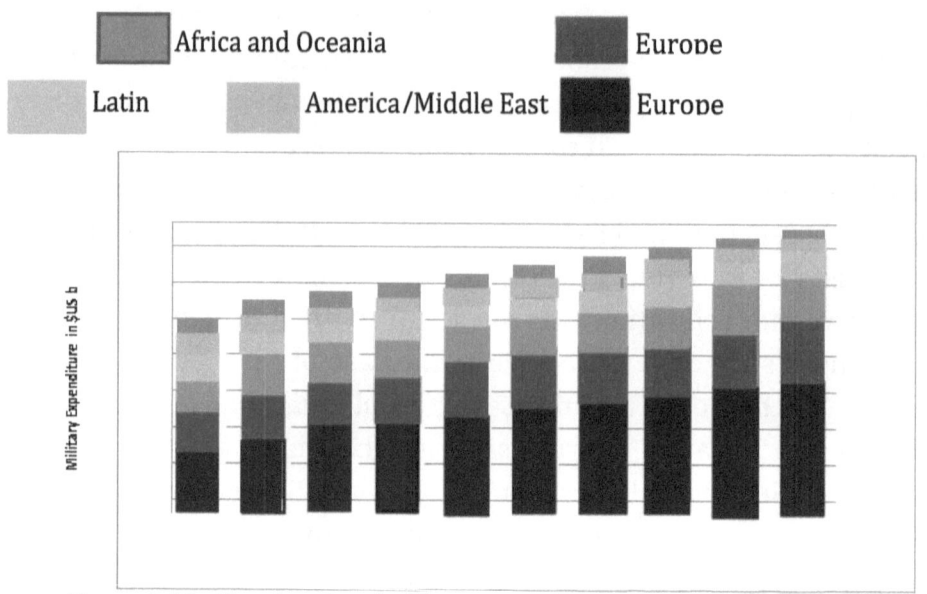

Figure 1. World and regional military expenditure estimates, 2000–2009

From the first three among these regions in the chart above, we saw that the revenue from natural resources played a significant role in the determination of both the dynamics and level of military spending in many countries. More so, we see that this revenue has often contributed to a rapid increase in military spending in recent years. In 2009, there was a slow trend of military spending in some cases due to the fall in prices of commodities as a result of the world economic crisis.

THE IMPACT OF THE NIGER DELTA CONFLICT, THE AMNESTY PROGRAMME AND THE RISE IN MILITARY EXPENDITURE ON THE ECONOMIC GROWTH OF NIGERIA.

This section is focused on the rapid rise in Nigeria's military spending as a function of the rise in oil revenue, the Niger Delta conflicts, the Amnesty Programme and its effect on the economic growth of Nigeria. Over the past decades, there has been an expansion in the global economy which has kept the demand and prices of oil and gas high and as such, increasing income and providing investment opportunities for African countries that are rich in energy and natural resources. This has also helped them to shape the level of their military spending. Since the extraction of oil can fuel violent conflict, then it is imperative to secure and protect production which is often the reason for an increase in military expenditure[53]. Examples of countries whose oil revenues have influenced their military expenditure are Nigeria, Algeria, Angola and Chad. In 2008, Nigeria was the largest exporter of crude oil in Africa and the 13th largest in the world, so the government's revenue from the sale of oil and gas accounted for 81 percent of the country's income.

From 2000 – 2008, revenue from the sale of oil and gas contributed to the high economic growth of the nation with an average growth rate of 7.7 percent annually which in turn contributed to the rapid rise in military spending. In 2009, the official military expenditure was estimated to be 224 billion Naira ($1.5billion), which is a 4.0 percent increase in real terms compared with 2008 and 101 percent from 2000. Nigeria's military expenditure figure is said to be significantly underestimated as a result of the sensitive secrecy in

---

53 CollierandHeoffler, (2004)

the military, weak budgetary system and poor management of the oil revenue by government institutions. Military operations conducted by the Federal Government to protect the production of crude oil in the Niger Delta region has significantly increased the Federal Government's military expenditure due to a rise in internal security challenges since 1999. Among them is the internal conflict and insurgency in the Niger Delta region that disrupted the crude oil production. Due to the high demand for oil and gas in the global economy, the Nigerian Government has increased its military expenditure by the purchase of recent and sophisticated ammunition to combat insurgency and other internal security challenges in the country.

The government uses the increased income from oil revenue to make extra funding for the military because of the important role and influence of the military in politics.

The Nigerian Government, since 2000, has spent a substantial part of her budget on the purchase of aerial surveillance systems, new patrol boats for military patrol in the waterways by the navy, fighter jets and helicopters for the air force and 193 cobra armoured vehicles for the army. The increase in oil income in Nigeria, has no doubt, generated economic growth, increased the importance of crude oil infrastructures but also increased insurgency, agitation and grievances in the Niger Delta region and vastly increased the military spending to curb and forestall internal and external security challenges and to protect and secure crude oil production in the region. Since 1966 when the first civil conflict broke out in the region, there have been consistent and continuous militant attacks against multinationals' oil pipeline installation and government infrastructural facilities by militants operating in the region and which has had a negative impact on the nation's economic growth owing to the fact that the nation gets more than 70 percent of her income from crude oil exploration and exportation. No country can record any significant economic growth in the midst of insecurity, conflicts, civil unrest etc. because it will erode the confidence of potential investors that would want to invest in the economy.

As such, they will either change their mind from investing in such a volatile environment or if they already had investments, would resolve to take their investment portfolio from such a risky business environment to a place that is business-friendly and characterised by a considerable level of the security of their investment, thereby hampering the growth of the economy. A peaceful, friendly and secure business environment is a necessary condition and critical component for economic growth.

With the continuous rise of insurgency and militancy in the region, the Nigerian government has also increased its military spending for security purposes in the country, particularly in the regions of conflict. The increase in military expenditure also decreases the pace of economic growth in the country because scarce and limited economic resources are taken from a productive sector of the economy to fund unproductive military operations as they do not have a positive effect on the country's economic growth.[54] The Niger Delta conflict has triggered a number of macroeconomic variables. For example, such operations make government revenues vulnerable to external shocks and the increase in government expenditure. The increase in government expenditure is reflected in the increase in government spending on the military.

When compared to global standards, the investment on security and defence by African States are still considerably low even when the level of insecurity, political tension and economic instability are relatively high[55]. The security situations are the main factors and determinants of the increase in military spending. One of the main and important issues faced by developing countries is the challenge

---

[54] Villanueva,Knight,(Loayza;1996)
[55] Smaldone (2006)

posed by military spending because it really requires a lot of funds that are, most times, beyond the budget appropriated for military operations in the initial stage by the government. More as it is important for countries to have a considerable level of security so as to be able to curb and prevent internal and external threats to law and order, there is also an opportunity cost because the fund used to beef up more security could also be used for other important sectors that could speed up the pace of development. The opportunity cost of increased military spending cannot be overemphasised. For example, an increase in military spending may increase distortion thereby decreasing the efficient allocation of productive resources. Also, a rise in military spending can also decrease the total stock of resources that can be used for other alternative economic activities like the investment in technological advancement and innovation, investment in productive capital, portfolio management and investment in other productive capital like health, education, infrastructure etc.[56].

There is a continuous challenge to sustain per capita economic growth due to the rise in poverty, the revenue vulnerability to external shocks and the rapid population growth, as such, policy makers and researchers argue that there is an urgent need to promote a conducive and efficient macroeconomic environment for investments and economic growth and development. This urgent need was what prompted the Federal Government to initiate and grant the amnesty to the militants as an avenue to bring to an end the militancy and insurgency in the region and to create a conducive business-friendly environment for investors. Policy makers considered Amnesty Programme offered to the militants as one of the best policy choice and action that the government made because it did not only restore peace and normalcy in the region but it also

---

[56] Knight,LoayzaandVillianuva (1996)

reduced the military spending of the government to achieve peace by military operations, therefore enabling the government to reallocate the fund budgeted for military spending to other productive economic areas of the economy to increase production and output in the economy. Many scholars also argue that not all military spending in developing countries is always wasteful spending because expenditure on military training equips the military personnel with the adequate skills to contribute to the labour force of the economy. Military expenditure, to some extent, can be produced economically because it enhances and promotes the national security of the state and enforces property rights thereby providing an enabling environment for private investment to thrive thus, enhancing growth and output[57]. Many scholars have used cross-sectional growth regression to establish if there is a positive correlation between military spending and economic growth in the long run but the evidence and results were subject to criticism because they were mixed and inconsistent due to the empirical technique that was used.

A study revealed that there is no consistent statistically significant correlation between military spending and economic growth.[58] However, another study showed that there is a positive correlation between military spending and economic growth in a sample of 44 least developing countries (LDCs), using the Spearman Rank Order Regression between the 1950 and 1965 timeline[59]. One main problem that is usually faced when using the cross-country growth regression is that it does not take into account the dynamics of the relationship between the two variables, rather it disregards and omits the country-specific factors. Normal cross-sectional regression does not give an insight into the direction and point of the causality rather it focuses on associating the military spending

[57] Thompson(1974)
[58] BiswasandRam(1986)
[59] Benoit (1973, 1978)

and economic growth with other variables. Using the Cointegration and Error Correction model to study and determine the relationship between military spending and economic growth with a sample of 62 countries it was found that there is a causal relationship between military spending and economic growth among the countries[60]. This study also omitted other factors that are specified in each country.

NIGER DELTA AMNESTY, MILITARY SPENDING AND ECONOMIC GROWTH

In this part, I tried to determine the relationship between military spending due to the conflicts and the Amnesty Programme and economic growth in the Niger Delta region. Many scholars argued that granting of amnesty to the militants in the Niger Delta by the Federal Government did not only restore peace to the region but it also reduced military spending of the government in an attempt to restore peace and security in the region by force, through military operations. Many economists and social scientists widely believe that the reduction in military expenditure can improve a country's pace of economic growth and development. However, only a few studies have been carried out to substantiate this argument that there is a positive effect or correlation between military spending and economic growth in Nigeria, incorporating the Amnesty Programme in the region. In all the studies done to give a vivid explanation of the subject matter, there is still no general and acceptable view on the subject. In a survey conducted using 102 studies on the economic effect of military spending, the evidence in the result shows that almost 39% of the cross country studies and 35% of the case studies found a negative effect of military expenditure on economic growth while 20% of the results show that

---

[60] Dakurah et al (2001)

there is a positive effect of the two types of studies of military spending on economic growth[61].

Figure 2 shows the trend in military spending in Nigeria since 1988. The continuous and consistent increase in military spending can

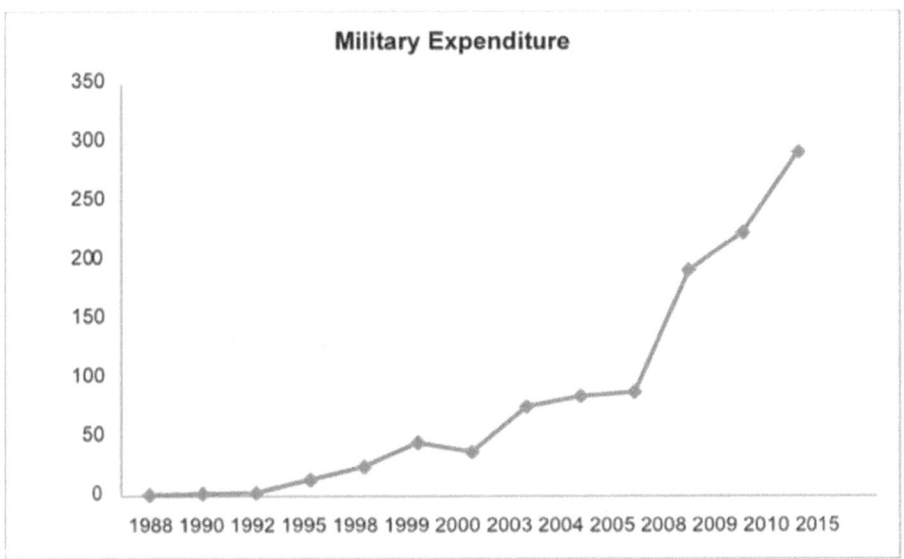

mostly be attributed to militancy and insurgency in the Niger Delta, internal and external conflicts and until recently, the terrorism and insurgency by Boko haram in the Northern part of Nigeria. Nigeria's military expenditure in 2010 is estimated to be about 292 Billion Naira (see *Table 1*). This is more than the average budget of each Niger Delta State annually.

Figure 2 shows the increase in military spending in billions from 1988 to 2010 prior to 2011, the year that the Federal Government granted amnesty to the militants. As shown from the diagram above, there was a systematic increase in military spending from 1988 to 1999. This is the period of the military regime when militants were suppressed by the military government. From 1999 until 2000,

---

[61] Dunne and Uye (2009)

there was a little decrease in military spending because Nigeria just elected their leaders through a democratic process and the militants were very hopeful that their elected leaders and representatives would work to meet the needs and aspirations of the Niger Delta people, as such, they decided to put a temporary stop to the conflicts. This was one of the major reasons for the decrease in 2000.

Between 2000 to 2003, there was a slight increase because 2003 was another election year and it is often believed the election period often triggered civil unrest and internal crisis because politicians often armed their loyalists to rig elections for them, as such, the government usually tried as much as possible to beef up security in order to curb crisis during the election period. Between 2005 and 2010, military spending increased drastically to tune of 292 billion Naira. This rapid increase was due to the upgrade of military equipment, training of military personnel abroad and the purchase of new and sophisticated military jet bombers, gunboats for military patrol in the waterways and armoured vehicles. The Federal Government increased military spending during this period to be able to tackle the rising conflicts and insurgency by the militants in the Niger Delta region and the emergence of terrorism by Boko Haram in the Northern part of Nigeria. The government did everything that could be done to ensure that it keeps the security situation in check to prevent the disintegration of the country into anarchy. It was also to ensure that the country was safe for its citizens and foreign investors to carry out their business without any form of fear.

The military spending was systematically rising as the conflict and insurgency by the militants in the Niger Delta region and the terrorists in the North were rising and this rise also led to an increase in the total public expenditure thereby slowing the pace of economic growth since limited resources were being used to finance military operations and crisis prevention.

PUBLIC SPENDING AND CONFLICT

There have been a recent number of works done to establish the role and significant importance of government public spending in crisis prevention. Basically, there are three types of government public spending namely:

- General Government Expenditure;

- Government Expenditure on the Military;

- Government Expenditure on Social Amenities, Infrastructure and Social Security Services.

In this section, I emphasise government expenditure on social amenities and its effect on the prevention of crisis. The primary cause of civil conflict in most African countries is as a result of the failure of the government to make a public expenditure to meet the basic needs of the people such as education, health and security. A game-theoretical model that explicitly established the correlation between redistributive policy adopted by the state and domestic peace in the society was used to validate the finding[62]. A strong and effective redistributive policy and programme that takes into account the people's basic needs will definitely guarantee a considerable level of peace and quietness in the society. When the government undertakes programmes and adopts policies that are community based and focused on the people's needs, for example, by increasing spending on quality, affordable and effective health care services and educational system, security and protection of lives and properties etc., it does not only prevent the risk of conflict occurrences but it also shows that the government cares about the

---

[62] Azam(2001)

people and are concerned about the ultimate wellbeing of the society which they govern.[63]

When the government adopts social welfare policies and make public spending on social welfare programmes its priority, it will lead to more cooperation, loyalty and support from the citizens and it will prevent civil unrest and conflict and make it difficult and impossible for rebel groups to operate[64]. The benefits that the government stands to gain if they adopt a social welfare policy that has a positive impact on the standard of living of her citizens through an effective and strong redistributive system that mainly focuses on the poor are, enormous. Some of the benefits are that it gains support and cooperation from a wide segment of the population. Political opposition decreases, the incentive and motivation for rebel groups to organise rebellion vanishes and it will also become difficult and impossible for those disadvantaged members of the society to take up arms to cause any form of civil unrest since they can afford the basic things of life without much pressure from the society. The redistributive system that focuses on the poor was the strategy that was used by many Western rulers in the 19th century to prevent conflict, social unrest, and to gain more support, cooperation and loyalty from their subjects and most importantly to establish and increase their legitimacy as leaders in the society[65].

The legitimacy of any government is subject to the condition only and if only it meets the daily and fundamental needs of its citizens[66]. Agreeably, government investments on human capital and social spending promote economic growth and development because it has a positive influence on labour opportunities, the distribution of

---

[63] Stasavage, (2005)
[64] TaydasandPeksen(2012)
[65] Acemoglu and Robinson, (2000)
[66] Robin (2012)

earning capacities and social mobility which are the major factor for economic growth and development[67].

Social spending can lead to better skilled acquisition which increases the efficiency and productivity of workers in their workplace and it enhances the global competitiveness of the economy[68]. Civil unrest and violent conflict will decrease when the quality of life of the people is improved and when wealth is promoted in the society through an effective social welfare policy adopted by the state.

THE ROLE OF EDUCATION ON CONFLICT PREVENTION

Scholars agree that education creates opportunities for economic growth and development, promotes social equality and decreases the grievances and agitation that usually causes civil unrest and social conflict in the society. One of the main grievances for the cause of the 22 year long civil war in Sudan was the failure and inability of the Sudanese Government to provide adequate, quality and affordable educational resources for the Southern Region[69]. The war in Sierra Leone by rebels can also be traced to the failure of the Sierra Leonean Government to adequately provide education in the society[70]. Similarly, at the micro level, the result of the interview conducted by experts with young soldiers showed strong evidence that lack of education and poverty with little or no income

---

[67] (Korpi and Palme, 1998; Chu, Davoodi and Gupta, 2000; Justino, 2003, Rudra, 2004; Thyn 2006).
[68] (Burgoon, 2006; Avelino, Brown and Hunter 2005; Brown and Hunter 2004; Gupte and Verhoeven, 2001; King, 1998; Van de Walle 1996; Schultz, 1963)
[69] Glickman (2000), Deng (2001) and Breidlid (2005)
[70] Richards (2003)

alternative opportunities are the major rationales for joining rebel groups. [71]

Also, it was found that most youths that participate in the armed struggle in the Niger Delta conflict for the agitation and control of local resources are those youths who have little or no form of educational training[72]. Education can promote and sustain social order and cohesion thereby encouraging the student to develop and cultivate the required interpersonal skills to seek legitimate means to resolve disputes amicably and such social cohesion can enable the state to achieve economic and social stability[73]. While on the other hand, it reduces the chances of violent conflict. Education widens and broadens the view of people thereby making them tolerant of other members of the society and as such decreases extremist ideologies and activities and increases the people's ability to pursue their needs, interest and aspirations using a legitimate political process[74].

Education also provides the opportunity for people to acquire the relevant civil skills to increase their political participation and to attain social stability and maintain law and order.

---

[71] Brett and Specht (2004)
[72] Oyefusi(2008)
[73] Thyne (2006),
[74] Lipset (1959)

CHAPTER THREE

THE CONCEPT AND RESPONSES TO RESOURCE CONTROL IN NIGERIA

The idea of resource control is the ownership and management of the resources of the region where they are located for the overall benefit of the region. The struggle and agitation for resource control is a critical and contending issue in the Niger Delta conflict.

From the responses in the key informant's sample, the Niger Delta people are agitating for the full control of their God-given resources for the development of the region. Other responses argue that if the Federal Government cannot afford to give them full control of their resources, they should be given full participation and the greater portion of the proceeds from the oil resources should be allocated to them and be used for the development of the region. An interviewee puts it this way,

'Resources control means giving the region where the resources are located the right to fully participate as a major stakeholder in the ownership, management and distribution of the resources in the region because, when they

are included in the ownership and management of the region, it gives them a sense of belonging and it gives the region higher chances to benefit from the proceeds of the oil resources in terms of development'.

Table 3

The table below shows the responses of the respondents in the key informant sample:

	Rivers	Bayelsa	Delta	Total
Claiming ownership of what belongs to the region	1 (6.67)	5(25%)	8 (40)	16(29.1)
Directing and controlling own resources	10(66.67)	4(20%)	1(05)	8(14.5)
Controlling and managing resources for self-development	4 (26.66)	11(55%)	11 (55)	31(56.4)
Total	**15**	**20**	**20**	**55**

From the result of the sample, we can see that the idea of resource control is viewed from the situation where the Federal Government will give back the ownership and control of the resources of the region to the people in the region and then make the region to pay a certain amount as tax to the Federal Government from the proceeds of the oil resources. This indicates true Federalism as it is done in the United States of America. As one correspondent said,

'There will be no equity, fairness and justice except the Federal Government practices true Federalism and hands over the ownership, control and management of the resources to the people in the region'.

From the correspondents, it is obvious that the Niger Delta people want complete control of their resources and they believe the region will continue to experience conflict as a result of the agitation except the Federal Government gives them total ownership, control and management of their resources.

Table 4

The table below shows the reason for the agitation for resource control and the effect which resulted in conflicts in the region.

Problems and Causes	Rivers	Bayelsa	Delta	Total
Poor Governance and Leadership	6(6.74)	-	5(5.88%)	10(3.98)
High Level Unemployment	6(6.74%)	10(12.99%)	11(12.94%)	28(11.16)
Marginalisation	16(17.98%)	4(5.196%)	2(2.35%)	22(8.76)
Lack of development/ Neglect by Federal Government	15(16.85%)	22(28.57)	38(44.71)	75(29.88%)
Economic Exploitation and Deprivation	18(26.22%)	22(28.57)	18(21.18%)	58(23.10%)
Disdain of the Minority Ethnic Groups	18(20.22%)	4(5.19%)	2(2.35%)	24(9.56%)
No Resource Control	10(14.495)	15(19.48%)	9(10.59)	34
Total	89	77	85	251

From the samples about the opinion and perception of the Niger Delta people in terms of resource control, we observed that the Niger Delta people want adequate attention and recognition from the Federal Government and full participation as a major stakeholder of the resources it produces, adequate development of the region and fair representation in the management processes of the resources of the Niger Delta. They seek fairness, justice and equitable treatment of its people as a minority ethnic group.

Dateline: Wednesday, July 11, 2018

It was an unusual experience for the staff and guests at Eko Hotels and Suites, located in the highbrow Victoria Island, Lagos, as a sea of influential Niger Delta indigenes, including top traditional rulers, religious and opinion leaders, intellectuals, community and youth leaders filed into the Main Hall of the hotel at noon. They were all at the venue in response to a call by the Special Adviser to the President on Niger Delta and Coordinator, Presidential Amnesty Programme (PAP), Prof. Charles Quaker Dokubo, to rub minds on how to deepen peace in the hitherto volatile Niger Delta region and pave way for socio-economic development. By 2p.m, when the stakeholders' meeting which had 153 delegates in attendance eventually kicked-off, it was clear the Niger Delta region was headed for better days.

With a thumb-up for initiators of the Amnesty Programme for ex-agitators, Dokubo noted that the prevailing peace in the region is indicative of the successes so recorded by the Amnesty Programme, which has made the Niger Delta region the most peaceful part of the country and one conducive for development. His words were,

---

'I am exceedingly grateful to God Almighty for making this day possible. I have really been looking forward to this family meeting. It is therefore with immense joy that I welcome all of you... Since inception, the Amnesty Programme, to a reasonable extent, has achieved its core mandate of aiding the processes of building and sustaining peace and safety in the Niger Delta and the entire Gulf of Guinea. I am not saying that we have attained perfection or an Eldorado of sorts; I am only

saying that the situation could have been far worse in the region and of course for the economy of our dear country. I do not believe that there is anyone here who is not aware that prior to the proclamation of unconditional amnesty for former agitators in the Niger Delta in 2009, disruptions in the exploration, processing and export of crude oil almost brought our economy to a standstill. Unfortunately, Nigeria's economy largely depends on earnings from oil exports, hemorrhaged very badly during this sad era of militancy. I have since found out that the situation got so bad that on a particular day in 2008, Nigeria was only able to produce 700,000 barrels of crude oil. Today, owing to the success of the Amnesty Programme, Nigeria is now able to meet its current OPEC Quota of 2.2 Million Barrels per day. We must all thank, most profusely, the ex-agitators in the Niger Delta who have continued to keep the peace in accordance with the pact they entered into with the Federal Government after accepting the offer of amnesty. Kudos must also go to you our traditional, religious, opinion, intellectual and community leaders as well as the leaderships of ethnic nationalities and youth groups in the Niger Delta. If you did not show leadership, persons enlisted in the Presidential Amnesty Programme may well have derailed. So, topmost among the reasons why I have called this meeting is to, on behalf of President Muhammadu Buhari and the Federal Government of Nigeria, thank you all most sincerely for the critical roles you have all continued to play either as individuals or groups to help sustain and even deepen peace in the Niger Delta.

'I chose to regard the Niger Delta as a work-in-progress and I am happy to inform the leaders of the region assembled here that the ultimate goal of the administration of President Muhammadu Buhari is to achieve sustainable development in all facets of the

63

region. Indeed, previous administrations at the federal level easily cited the absence of a "conducive environment" for not developing the Niger Delta. The good news is that speaking about peace, safety and security, I daresay that the Niger Delta is perhaps the most conducive region for development in Nigeria today. Our great nation has everyone in this hall to thank for this'.

Dokubo said from findings and recommendations of a committee he constituted on assumption of office to review the Amnesty Programme, as well as his interactions with key stakeholders, including the leadership of the ex-agitators, he mapped out his priority, which included the completion and activation of all the vocational training centres under construction across the states in the Niger Delta to fast track the training of the several beneficiaries awaiting skills acquisition, and empowerment through the provision of start-up packs and mentoring for several of the already trained and qualified ex-agitators to become entrepreneurs and possibly employ others.

Also dear to his heart, is the sanitisation of the Education Department of the Amnesty Office to make it more impactful and cost-effective; restoring the certainty and sanctity of the database of the Presidential Amnesty Programme with strong measures in place to deter and forestall future breaches; holding regular consultative meetings with the Programmes' critical stakeholders, and effective liaison with governments of the states in the Niger Delta with a view to creating platforms for gainful employment for already trained ex-agitators.

Before drawing the curtains open for questions, he gave an insight into some salient issues bothering on the unending clamour for the enlistment of more persons into the Amnesty Programme, operations of the Amnesty Office and terminal date for the programme.

'Since assuming office as the Coordinator of the Presidential Amnesty Programme, I have spent quality time studying all documents I have been able to lay my hands on regarding the Amnesty Programme and I have decided to address three critical issues that tend to confound or confuse even the most knowledgeable stakeholders of the Programme. Out of the 30,000 persons enlisted in the Presidential Amnesty Programme, 11,297 persons are still in the queue, waiting to be placed in either vocational training facilities or sent to tertiary institutions for formal education. However, permit me to clarify here and now that I have also since found out that the Coordinator of the Amnesty Programme has no powers whatsoever to include even one person in the Amnesty Programme.

'The power of further inclusions resides with His Excellency, the President and Commander-in-Chief of the Armed Forces alone. Let me also further clarify that the enlistment in the Programme was largely based on the number of arms and ammunition returned to the Federal Government within a stipulated period. Enlistment into the Amnesty Programme was not done on a state-by-state basis. I have heard some people ask why a particular state or one ethnic group has more persons in the programme than the other. The simple answer is that enlistment was done by the personnel of the Armed Forces of Nigeria during the amnesty window based on the number of weapons surrendered by the ex-agitators irrespective of their states of origin or the ethnic nationality they come from'.

Expectedly, at the end of the meeting, participants rose to the brim with smiles, convinced that Dokuba had charted a lofty path for the Amnesty Programme. Pastor Power Aginighan, a former acting managing director of the Niger Delta Development Commission (NDDC), described the event as novel.

'Dokubo's initiative of holding the meeting is a most commendable move. For a personality who occupies a very strategic position in Nigeria at a time when there is a disconnect between those in government and those who are being governed, what he has done is bridging the gap and it is commendable', he said.

Ambassador Godknows Ighali, an ex-federal Permanent Secretary and Presidential Adviser, echoes Aginighan. Describing Dokubo's initiative as fantastic, he said the Amnesty Programme has had several Coordinators since inception but none had deemed it necessary to organise such an event.

King Alfred Diete Spiff, a former military governor of old Rivers State, the Paramount Ruler of Twon Brass Kingdom and Chairman, Bayelsa State Council of Traditional Rulers, says Dokubo hit the ground running.

'In my capacity as Chairman of a Chieftaincy Council, I will table this before my council later this month when we have our monthly meetings'.

Senior Special Assistant to the President on Economic Matters, Edobor Iyamu, hailed Dokubo for his commitment, 'His emphasis during the meeting seemed to be in the area of vocational training and retraining. All of these, no doubt, will address a lot of issues in the

---

Definitely, it is not yet Uhuru for the people of Niger Delta, but leaders of the area say they have seen light at the end of the tunnel of the Presidential Amnesty Programme. Their optimism is true, not misplaced.

CHAPTER FOUR

THE BUHARI ADMINISTRATION IMPACT ON THE NIGER DELTA

When the Buhari Administration assumed office on 29th May 2015, there were enormous uncertainties about his agenda for the Niger Delta region. Many prominent chiefs in the region were hopeful that maybe there will be a fresh start towards the development of the region and while others were very skeptical and unsure about what the political agenda of the newly elected president was. It is true that the president has demonstrated in the past, his unflinching support, and unwavering commitment to his tribe and his indisputable loyalty to the Northern region, most people in the Niger Delta region that voted for him in 2015 did so because of his proven but controversial track record of his fight against corruption as a military head of state between 1983 – 1985. When General Buhari took over power and overthrew the then democratically elected president, Shehu Shagari, he was able to justify his action by accusing the civilian government of a staggering level of corruption and a grossly flawed democracy. While most Nigerians strongly disagreed with the idea of overthrowing a civilian elected government that had just started building a democratic process, they were able to overlook the coup and accept that it was a necessity if that is the only way to deal with the corruption epidemic that has eaten deep into every fabric and civil life of the country.

The Niger Delta people voted for him because they were extremely tired of the status quo in the region. While they recognised that the previous administration under the leadership of President Goodluck Jonathan, a Niger Delta native, an indigene and son of the soil, tried his best toward the development of the region, they were unhappy about his leadership style as regards to fighting corruption in the region. They wanted someone who could be very aggressive in not only fighting the enormous corruption in the Niger Delta but also committed to cleaning up the stunning level of environmental pollution and degradation, aggressively addressing the continual causes of the crisis in the region and be committed to rebuilding the region that they wished for. They were hopeful towards the abundant resources and materials that the region possesses. From Delta to Edo, from Akwa Ibom to Cross River and from Port Harcourt to Bayelsa States respectively, the people who felt abandoned, ignored and left out in things that matter to them, decided to take a chance and voted for the man who promised them hope, optimism and a positive change in their situation. During the inauguration, in his inaugural speech, when he said, '*I belong to nobody and I belong to everybody*', it resonated in them an assurance that Buhari will be committed to giving an equal commitment, towards the Niger Delta people who were very hopeful, that the long-awaited solution had finally come.

Besides the continuous crises in the region, the biggest and existential threat to the people in the region is the alarming level of pollution in the region caused primarily by the devastating oil spillage. According to the UN Environment Programme, multinational oil companies, e.g. Shell, and other oil companies operating in the region had systematically caused severe environmental damage in the region by contaminating about 1000 sq. km area of Ogoniland with severe and disastrous consequences for not only human lives and health, but also the wildlife and the whole environmental ecosystem. According to a UN report, the devastation, pollution and environmental degradation due to the oil spillage in the Niger Delta over the past 50 years will take up to 30 years to clean up for the land to return to its original state and will cost about $1 billion. The crises in the region is just a piece of the bigger problem. The pollution is not just a critical issue but also an existential threat to the region.

Fortunately for the region, President Muhammadu Buhari's number one task among many in his agenda was the authorisation of funds to carry out the implementation of the recommendations of the United Nations Environmental Programme especially as regards to the clean-up of Ogoniland and other areas in the region that have been severely devasted and completely damaged due to the oil spillage. This damage done to the region is not just about the health and wellbeing of the communities but also about their source of livelihood which led to constant lawlessness, criminal behaviour and activities, and crisis in the region. When citizens felt abandoned by the governments whose sole responsibility was to protect and provide the ecosystem for the society to thrive, they lost faith and hope in the government, and often took their fate into their own hand, to do anything and everything they deemed right to survive, which often led to the breakdown of law and order, civil unrest and economic sabotage such as the vandalisation of oil pipelines.

The Buhari Administration is not only committed to the economic and environmental wellbeing of the Niger Delta region but his administration has overwhelmingly supported and committed to keeping the Paris Agreement under the United Nations Framework Convention on Climate Change because he strongly believes having a clean, secure and safe planet is not just the right thing to do but it is a noble and worthy cause to stand for.

There is no doubt that there are also a lot of people in the region that strongly believe the President Buhari Administration has done little or nothing for the region while others believe that he still favours other parts of the country, e.g. the North, than the Niger Delta region that has and still contributes over 80% to the National income.

For example, the Ijaw Youth Council expressed their displeasure about what they considered a biased treatment towards the South-South and Southeast region while at the same time, the administration was embarking on development projects in the North. They argued that the policies and programmes of President Buhari was being more beneficial to the North and cited a recent example when the President, during the Federal Executive meeting, approved the sum of ₦19 billion for the construction of roads in the Northern and Western parts of the country at the same time he ignored roads in the South-South region that desperately needed to be repaired. Some of the examples are the Warri-Benin Road, the Benin-Ore Road, the Benin-Asaba Road, the East-West Road and Benin – Lagos Road. Most of these roads have become death traps due to the deplorable condition they are in. It has become practically impossible for road users to use the road without wasting unnecessary time, and sometimes lives, due to the dangerous potholes. Some even argue that the condition of the roads make it possible for armed bandits to rob them easily. They have called the attention of the administration to their unpleasant experiences, concerns and hope to see that the president actually follows through with his commitment to being for nobody but being for everybody. They want to see that the president does more for the region just like he has done in other regions. They argue that if the administration continues to ignore some of the challenges they have expressed, there is every likelihood that the relative peace and stability that the region has been experiencing in recent times may be unsustainable, which should be a grave concern for everyone.

There is no doubt that these concerns are legitimate and valid. It would be completely disingenuous, and grossly misleading for the administration to in any way, shape or form either by act of wilful omission or commission, ignore or continue to disregard and fail to address the region's legitimate concerns because doing so will not only make the people to completely lose hope in the government as they did in the previous administration but could also hamper development and progress towards sustainable peace in the region. Most people in the region believe that the government can do more if it is sincerely committed to building a better, sustainable and prosperous Niger Delta where the people actually feel and experience the dividend of their resources.

NOTABLE ACHIEVEMENTS OF BUHARI'S ADMINISTRATION IN THE NIGER DELTA

It is true that the administration still has a lot to do for the Niger Delta in order to alleviate the untold hardships toward economic prosperity in the region, it is also true that the administration has achieved some monumental achievements in the region to position it in the path of economic prosperity, sustainable growth, political stability and increase in security of the region.

1. The Ogoni Clean Up Project

    Based on the United Nations' report about the environmental damages caused by oil spillage and the time it would take to clean-up the area to start the rebuilding of the ecosystem and the soil to return to its original state, President Buhari approved and set aside $170 million (USD) to fund the clean-up of the Ogoniland. This project is under the Ministry of Environment and will be managed by the Hydrocarbon

Pollution Remediation Project (HYPREP). The Escrow Agreement was signed in April 2018 and an account called "The Escrow Account" was opened specially for the clean-up project. According to the United Nations reports, it will take about 30 years to clean up the communities that are affected by the pollution but like a famous philosopher once said, "A journey of a thousand steps begin with a single step". It is on this premise that the president began the groundwork of the cleaning process towards the better, cleaner and healthier region. Due to how long the project will take and the depth of expertise that is required to do the exceptionally complex work, the administration took for a very smart initiative to not only commit to the clean-up, but to also train graduates from Ogoniland and other affected areas who have a background in Environmental Science to acquire the required skillsets to increase their capacity and expertise to build the remediation framework of the project and to maintain and manage the project from the initiation phase to the closing phase. This approach is a long-term cost-saving strategy because it will enable the government to save resources that would have been used to get-in and hire expatriates, create job opportunities for the locals and also give the locals from the affected areas with an Environmental Science background the opportunity to acquire the skillsets that are required, develop the capacities to self-manage the project leading to a win-win situation. People of the region were very excited when the project was announced and it gave them a shared sense of relief, hope and optimism

2. The Establishment of the Nigerian Maritime University

The need for the establishment of a specialised university is long overdue. As the world is increasingly becoming globalised in a unique and complex way, the demand for specialised universities cannot be overemphasised. Organisations and companies are beginning to focus on employees that have a specialised set of skills that will be relevant in today's workplace. This is what made the Petroleum Training Institute, Effurun, Delta State stand out from the time it was established by President Olusegun Obasanjo when he was the military head of state in 1973. It was established specifically to train and equip people with the right skillsets, capacity and manpower to meet the labour for the demand of the Oil and Gas Industry in Nigeria and globally. The institute has an outstanding reputation and proven track record of meeting the labour force demand of companies in the oil and gas industry for more than four decades. Companies like Shell, Chevron and other Oil and Gas companies often recruit new hires from this institute because of the quality of graduates it produces. It could only be possible because it was established as a specialised institution whose mandate and objective are to meet a labour force demand in the Oil and Gas and Energy sector. They have been doing that successfully for the past forty years.

I believe that the region should have specialised degree-awarding institutions that will train people to have the required skill set that will make them stay competitive in the marine sector/industry because of the strategic location of the Niger Delta with its proximity to water bodies and its comparative advantage. This is why the establishment of the Nigerian Maritime University is a welcome development that the state in particular and the region in general needs in this ever-changing dynamic economy where the demand for specialised skillset is in high demand.

Due to the very challenging business environment, companies need to stay competitive and relevant so they are increasingly becoming more than ever laser-focused when it comes to hiring employees. They are not just looking for graduates with a degree in certain fields, rather they are focused on getting the right people with expertise in a particular industry and it is only specialised universities and institutions that are commissioned to offer certain specialised degrees that can meet the industry's demand for manpower. The Nigerian Maritime University located in Okorenkoko, Delta State, is established to train Maritime experts to deal with the challenges that are usually faced in the Maritime industry, not only in the Niger Delta region but also in Nigeria and globally. Through the bold leadership of President Buhari, the Nigeria Maritime University, Okerenkoko, Delta State, was initiated and it took off as a full degree awarding institution and it is entitled all the privileges and status of all other federal universities in the country. The National Universities Commission gave full approval for the institution to commence undergraduate degree programmes that took effect in the 2017/2018 academic session. The president officially approved a take-off grant of about ₦5 billion and also approved an additional ₦1 billion to begin the recruitment of academic and non-academic staff and the building of the important infrastructural projects. On 12th April 2018, the university officially started academic activities. This monumental accomplishment is not just a political scorecard for the administration but also an enormous win for Delta State, in particular, and the Niger Delta region, in general. This academic achievement will create job opportunities for locals, create an opportunity to be trained and empowered to become better and responsible citizens, and to make a lasting and positive impact in the communities. This is a laudable achievement of this administration and it should be highly commended.

3. The Building of the Ogoni Health Outreach

Ogoniland is where everything began, so there is nothing that will be too much which the President can do. This is the place that was severely devastated by environmental pollution from the unethical operations of multinational corporations who place profit above the wellbeing of the host communities. Their livelihood was not only gone because their water was polluted, their fishing business died because the fishes died due to chemical pollution from the oil spillage and they were literally unable to have access to clean and healthy water for their daily use. Due to the pollution of their water, their health was severely affected and in some rare cases, some developed asthma while others developed other complicated health challenges. In line with the report and recommendation of the United Nations Environment Programme, the Buhari Administration initiated, established and kicked off the Ogoni Health Outreach Program to aggressively address the various health challenges of the locals caused by the pollution. Since the programme was flagged off, more than 60 surgical cases and complex health-challenges have been treated and over 550,000 have been treated for various health challenges. As the President said, he is committed to a better, cleaner, safer and healthier Niger Delta because an economically prosperous region can also be possible and achievable if the people are living in a better, cleaner and healthier environment.

4. A Renewed Commitment Toward the Sustainability of the Presidential Amnesty Programme

While it cannot be disputed that the Presidential Amnesty Programme was initiated by the previous administration (initially the Yar'adua/ Jonathan Administration) and actually led to relative peace in the region, the President's administration strongly believed that the positive impact of the Presidential Amnesty Program should be sustained to continue and maintain relative peace and stability in the region. In the light of continuing with the peaceful, rehabilitation, training and reinstating agenda for the previous administration, this administration is also committed to continuing the programme because evidence shows that the programme actually worked and was successful toward the peaceful rebuilding of the region. For example, in the 2016 budget, President Buhari approved an additional ₦35 billion for the Amnesty Programme to continue the rehabilitation to sustain and manage the reintegration programme of the ex-militants and ex-agitators of the region. There is no doubt that his programme has unquestionably led to relative peace in the region. Another bold step this administration continues to take toward the continuity of building capacities and ensuring indigenes of the region are better equipped to become responsible citizens is, the unwavering commitment to continue to ensure that indigenes from the communities affected in the region, benefit from full academic scholarship to access quality education with a monthly stipend. The goal is to ensure that the region has highly trained and qualified people to help contribute to the overall development and wellbeing of their communities as responsible citizens of those communities.

5. The Establishment of Modular Refineries

It is not uncommon to see the vandalisation of pipelines and the theft of crude oil and sometimes even refined petroleum products in some communities. Sometimes, such activities are perpetuated by some youths in the communities either because they are driven by greed or as a sign of protest against the companies that own or manage the pipelines, or to express their anger and displeasure as a result of the felt marginalisation by the Federal Government. While this behaviour is deemed criminal in the eyes of the law, they usually argue to justify their actions that it is the only way to call the attention of the Federal Government to their plight. However, no matter how genuine or well-intentioned their reasons are, it is still a criminal behaviour that not only causes monetarily losses to the companies and the Federal Government, but also poses an environmental danger to the host communities and potential death of people who are involved in this heinous crime because of the likelihood of fire explosion. An example of this is the deadly explosion that killed over 1000 people on 18th October 1998 in a community called Jesse in Ethiope West Local Government Council of Delta State. This was the most horrific accident since the history of pipeline vandalisation in the Niger Delta region and till date, it is considered the most single explosion to take the most lives when compared to other pipeline explosions in the history of Nigeria. While the exact cause of the explosion was subjected to debate at that time, the Nigerian Government strongly believed and stated that the explosion was a result of the vandalisation of the pipeline by criminals. Bodies were burned beyond recognition and the scene was terrifying to behold. It was like hell broke loose. The explosion was so severe that it took days for it to be contained with the help of fire servicemen from the United States. Other fire explosions have happened in different communities of the country. There was a pipeline explosion near Lagos State in September 2014 when some people tried to damage pipes and siphon crude oil from it which resulted in the death of 50 people. Another eminent pipeline explosion that took over a hundred lives occurred in December 2006 when a pipeline carrying petroleum products was vandalised by some people at midnight. These incidents often occurred from time to time but stakeholders believe that the establishment of modular refineries in some of these communities can significantly reduce the chances of pipeline vandalisation thereby eliminating these avoidable deaths caused by this criminal behaviour. Based on their insight and recommendation, the Buhari Administration approved the establishment of Modular Refineries in all the states in the Niger Delta and issued a total of 38 licenses for medium to high-scale refineries that can conveniently produce between 50,000 to 250,000 barrels per day. Stakeholders believe this bold initiative and bold step taken by the administration has indeed contributed to the decline in the vandalisation rates of oil pipeline in the region and actually commended the administration for paying attention to their plight and taking a step to address this socio-economic menace in the region. In addition to the issuance of a license to establish Modula refineries, the administration also established a community-based security framework where the oil pipelines and other oil and gas assets are contracted and protected by indigenous companies in the region. The Modular refineries will also be able to create and improve the capacity to domestically refine petroleum product that are necessary to meet the exceeding demand the NNPC couldn't meet and also reduce the proliferation of unlicensed and illegal refineries in the black market in the region.

6. Commitment to Agriculture and Food Sufficiency in the Region

No one was surprised to see the commitment of this administration toward building and revamping the agriculture sector in Nigeria to ensure an effective and efficient food sufficiency because President Buhari is also a farmer. He knows the importance of having a vibrant agriculture sector in the country. Before the discovery of crude oil in the 1950s, Nigeria's economy was based on agriculture and used to be a major producer of palm oil from the South and groundnut from the North. Kano was known for the famous Groundnut Pyramid. The president has made it clear that making Nigeria self-sufficient on food production is one of his top priorities and fortunately, the Niger Delta has benefited from his robust agenda to revamp the agriculture sector. The president established the Presidential Initiative which is entirely focused to revamp and boost the Agriculture Industry across the nine states in the Niger Delta region. Some of the benefits of his agenda are the establishment and completion of six cassava processing plants in Imo, Cross River, Bayelsa, Ondo, and Rivers states respectively. More than 700 women and youths have been adequately trained and have acquired the required skillsets to venture into various agricultural businesses namely; crop production, aquaculture and poultry and at the end of their training, they were given ₦1 million naira to start their small-medium size agro-business. Over 200 women that specialised in snail farming, fish farming and poultry production were given about ₦350,000 to ₦500,000 each, to empower them to start their dream business. Also, about 240 women and youths in the region were trained in a non-agriculture sector such as ICT and other technical skills like repairing phones and other vocational training. This administration understands that one of the ways to put the economy on the fast track toward economic prosperity and socio-political stability in the region is to not only engage them but also empower them to be self-employed so that these people can be co-partners in the building process towards a prosperous nation. By engaging and empowering indigenes in these communities, there has been a significant decline in criminal activities, the multiplier effect of job creation and an increase in the socio-political stability in the region. When people feel empowered to achieve their personal and economic goals, they become disinterested in any form of criminal-like behaviour.

7. Commercialisation of Gas Flaring

Nigeria is one of the few countries in the world that still flares its gas into the air. Gas flaring is not just a waste of vital resources but also contributes to the pollution of the air. This is a time when there is the call for countries to cut down their carbon emission and other environmental pollutants due to the increasing rate of devastation witnessed across countries over the world as a result of climate change. As Buhari stated in the meeting with the United Nations Environment Programme concerning his administration, he was committed to a cleaner and healthier environment, he took a bold step to address the environmental challenges of gas flaring that has been polluting the environment for many decades. The establishment of the Commercialisation of Nigerian Gas Flaring Programme was aimed to address these environmental challenges of gas flaring in the region and to build a road map of initiating the process of converting the gas flares into other resources as recommended by experts. This programme will not only play a significant role in reducing the environmental impact of the emissions but also to create an opportunity to convert the gas that has been wasted for decades to other useful resources. The programme will also create job opportunities for those who will be trained to get the required skillsets to perform the gas conversion process making it not only a smart and strategic policy move by the administration, but also a win-win situation towards a greener, cleaner and healthier economy.

8. The Flag Off of the Bonny-Bodo Road Project

Under the leadership of the President Buhari administration, the Bonny-Bodo Road Project was flagged off with about ₦120billion in October 2012 represented by the Vice President, Prof. Yemi Osinbajo, SAN. The project was jointly funded by the Nigerian Government and Nigeria LNG under a Public-Private Partnership Programme with each party paying 50% of the total cost of the N120 billion. The Bonny-Bodo Bridge and the road project is a 34-kilometre road and when completed, it would link and connect various major communities in the Niger Delta region and boost socio-economic activities and development in the region.

9. The Establishment of the Export Processing Zone

There has been a call to expand the Export Processing Zone in the country, particularly to reduce congestion in Lagos and enable goods exported or imported to be cleared in other locations in the country. President Buhari did listen to the concerns of the stakeholders and took an initiative to approve the establishment of another Export Processing Zone that consists of the Gas City Project at Ogidigben and the Deep Seaport in Gbaramatu, in Warri South-West Local Government Area in Delta State. The aim of this process is to increase and expand the number of Export Process Zones in the country, and because of the location of the Niger Delta and its proximity to the sea, it will enable importers and exporters doing business in the Niger Delta region to be able to import, export or clear their goods directly in the region instead of travelling to Lagos to clear them. It will save a lot of cost of transporting their goods from Lagos, reduce unnecessary travel, as well as boost the socio-economic activities in the region which will lead to the creation of more job opportunities. The establishment of the Export Processing Zone in the region was long overdue and it is highly commendable for the President to take this bold step to address some of these overdue concerns.

10. Challenges of Access to Funding Addressed

Due to the lack of access to financial credit for small and medium-sized farmers, the Niger Delta Region Development Management Board has stepped in to address the challenges of accessing financial and credit facilities by farmers in the region and they have taken the initiative to partner with other stakeholders to provide funding for the training of over 9000 farmers and also provide 10,000-hectares of farmland in the nine states of the region. The Agriculture programme is estimated to have created over 80,0000 new jobs in three years since it has been in operation.

While there are conflicting arguments about how the Buhari Administration has treated the Niger Delta region, it will be intellectually dishonest and factually inaccurate to argue that his administration has done nothing for the region.

Personally, I was not for President Buhari before his election and I still have divergent views as it relates to his policy and style of governance which I sometimes criticise, especially for his high handedness in regard to the Rule of Law, democratic principles and institutions but that does not in any way, make me undermine, ignore or deny the work he has done so far and continues to do for the Niger Delta people. Yes, there are still challenges facing the region that he is yet to address. Of course, there are still several steps he ought to take and I strongly believe he should continue to look at the critical issues that are important to the wellbeing and economic prosperity of the region. Nevertheless, we cannot wilfully deny or ignore the fact that he has achieved some major milestones in the region and these deserve to be recognised and commended.

CHAPTER FIVE

SUMMARY, CONCLUSION AND RECOMMENDATIONS

SUMMARY

In this book, *Economics of Conflict and Resource Control*, I argued that the root cause of the conflict in the region is due to the Federal Government's gross neglect, exploitation and marginalisation of the region which brought about the emergence of the agitation and struggle for resource control which was seen as the only legitimate means to get the attention of the Federal Government. The Niger Delta people want to control and manage their God-given resources and they want to participate as major stakeholders in every decision-making process that involves the control, management and distribution of their resources.

The agitation and struggle by the Niger Delta people for the control of their resources became necessary as a means, not only to get the attention of the Central Government but also a way to show their grievances against the economic deprivation, neglect and the adverse effects of oil exploitation on their environment and livelihood. The region wants the Federal Government to give them a fair, just and equitable share in the management and control of their resources and to accord them adequate development attention, recognition and participation in the processes that involve the control, management and distribution of their resources for the benefit of all.

The Niger Delta youths decided to confront this gross neglect to determine their own destiny after many years of frustration stemming from unemployment, poor living conditions, marginalisation and exclusion from developmental programmes of Nigeria in spite of the region's resource endowment and contribution to the national treasury. They decided to establish a platform where their voice will be heard and this gave rise to their struggles and militant agitations. This is because at some points, they lost confidence in the elders and leaders that are in the position to represent their interests and stand in dialogue with the Nigerian Government. The youths and militants in the region see themselves as freedom fighters as they channel their grievances against the injustice, exploitation and economic deprivation meted out to the inhabitants of the region with the purpose of reversing the trend and compelling the Federal Government to embark on developmental strides in the region. They used these agitations and struggles as a means to seek for the development and resource control of their region, especially concerning the youths in the region. Since it is widely said that the youths are the leaders of tomorrow, their efforts were to guarantee a better life, a safe and healthy environment and a secure future for them.

The conflict that emerged from the agitation and struggle for the resource control has, no doubt, had a severe impact not only on the Nigerian economy and its revenue, but also on the communities in the region, the youths, the stability and security of the region, inter-ethnic and communal relations, and the living conditions and livelihood of the Niger Delta people. From the analysis, we saw that the causes of the struggles, agitations and conflicts are due to the exclusion of the region in the scheme of things. Such processes that involve the control, management and distribution are the activities that the youths are clamouring to be involved in. Poverty and unemployment breed discontent, frustration and anger. Environmental pollution exacerbates poverty and unemployment. The nature of corporate and state governance particularly in relation to scanty developmental effort, insensitivity, failure to keep promises and agreements, and military suppression and repression, were seen as catalysing or provoking greater frustration, agitation, conflicts and violence in the region.

CONCLUSION

The conflicts started from peaceful protests and demonstrations to get the attention of the Central Government but escalated to a higher degree due to the consistent neglect and insensitivity to the plights of the Niger Delta people by the Nigerian Government and the multinational companies, whose continuous under-development, environmental pollution and degradation led to poverty and unemployment. These critical issues bred frustration in the region among the youths which led to protests and violent conflicts. On the other hand, the Federal Government and multinational companies, instead of engaging the youths in meaningful dialogue to hear them out and know the cause of their grievances so as to take appropriate measures on how to handle the situation amicably, resorted to the use of force, suppression and oppression through the military, police and other security to clamp them down. Unfortunately, this approach did not work as they thought. Rather, it escalated into the new wave of agitation, struggle and violent conflict. The youths resolved to challenge the state and counter the intimidation in a violent way thereby escalating the tense situation in the region.

The conflict in the region is basically a struggle for resource control and management. The individuals in the region, groups, communities, ethnic groups and the states in the region, elders, traditional elites, political societies and the youths are agitating and struggling to have access and control of the oil resources and its benefits. Resource control has taken different stages and levels with different methods of struggles to get the scarce resources. Host communities organised protests and traditional elites induced and manipulated the youths and used them to get benefits from the oil multinationals. Similarly, the militia and armed groups used force to compel benefits from the state and oil companies and also used force to appropriate oil resources through oil bunkering, vandalisation of oil pipelines, sabotage, theft and they lived on the proceeds they got from the sales.

RECOMMENDATIONS

For a conflict-free, peaceful and sustainable regional development to be achieved in the region, there is an urgent need to engage all stakeholders and economic agents in the region to take part in the processes that involve access to control, management and distribution of the oil resources in the region. The Federal Government should re-strategise the method of conflict management which has, so far, involved the use of force to repress the protesters from the oil-producing communities. Since this method has not yielded any meaningful and effective result in the past, but rather escalated the conflict to a higher level of violence, other more effective and peaceful methods should be adopted. This could be achieved through dialogue and compromise on both sides.

Also, the oil multinational companies should come up with better ways and means to address the critical issues that their host communities are facing, especially the environmental degradation that is usually caused by the oil exploitation and these measures should be incorporated into their business operations as a core and important issue that needs urgent attention. The prospect for a conflict-free, sustainable peace and development of the region requires a critical policy reorientation. An integrated bottom-up participatory process that secures the quality of life of the people and their psychological health, and simultaneously protects the environment is undoubtedly the path to a productive enterprise in the oil-producing communities. The youths should be motivated and mobilised for public participation and for political, social and economic empowerment. There should be a political commitment by the Federal Government and magnates of the oil industry to deliberately reverse the injustice done to the oil-producing areas and put the area back on the road to justice, stability and development.

Notes

REFERENCES

Albert, I. O. 2001. Building Peace, Advancing Democracy: Experience with Third-Party Interventions in Nigeria's Conflicts. Ibadan: John Archers.

Albert, I. O. 2003. The Odi Massacre in 1999 in the Context of the Graffiti Left by the Invading Nigerian Army. *PEFS Monograph New Series* No.1. Ibadan: John Archers.

African Network for Environment and Economic; Justice-Aneej .2004. *Oil of Poverty in Niger Delta*. Benin, Nigeria: ANEEJ.

Ashton-Jones, N. S. A.; Douglas, O. 1998. *The Human Ecosystems of the Niger Delta*. Benin City: ERA.

Abubakar, Shehu and Emmanuel Bello. 2004. 'I Resigned from the Nigerian Army to Join Dokubo—General Adedeji Ebo'. "The Political Economy of Illicit Small Arms Proliferation in Nigeria: Issues for a Human Security Agenda". Paper Presented as Part of the International Action Network on Small Arms (IANSA) Week of Action, Nigerian Defense Academy, Kaduna, June 2003

Aina, Akin Tada. 1996. "Globalization and Social Policy in Africa: Issues and Research Directions", Dakar, CODESRIA Working Paper Series, 6/96

Argenti, N. (1998). "Air Youth: Performance, Violence and the State in Cameroon," Journal of the Royal Anthropological Institute 4 (4): 753–81. British Columbus.' Weekly Trust (Abuja), 23–29 October, p. 17.

Bisina, J. (2006). "Environmental Degradation in the Niger Delta". Pambazuka News. Issue 281. http://pambazuka.org/en/category/comment/38728

Biswas, B. and Ram, R., 1986. Military Expenditures and Economic Growth in Less Developed

Benoit, E., 1973. Defence Spending and Economic Growth in Developing Countries. Lexington: Lexington Books.

Benoit, E. 1978. Growth and Defence in Developing Countries. Economic Development and Cultural Change. 26 (2): 271- 280. Countries: An Augmented Model and Further Evidence.

Economic Development and Cultural Change, 34, pp. 362-71.

Collier, P.; Hoeffler, A. 2002. "Greed and Grievance in African Civil Wars". CSAE Working Paper No. WPS/2002-01. Oxford: Centre for African Economies.

Collier, Paul. "Economic Causes of Civil Conflict and Their Implications for Policy." In Chester Connolly, M. and J. Ennew (eds.). 1996. "Children Out of Place," Childhood 3 (2): 131–45 CEDCOMS Monograph Series No. 1. Ile-Ife: Centre for Development and Conflict Management Studies

Crocker, Fen Osler Hampson and Pamela Aall, (eds). Leashing the Dogs of War.

Collier, Paul, and Anke Hoeffler. "Resource Rents, Governance, and Conflict." *Journal of Conflict Resolution* 49, no. 4 (2005): 625–633.

Du Nann Winter, Deborah, and Mario M. Cava. 2006. "The Psycho-Ecology of Armed Conflict." *Journal of Social Issues* 62, no. 1 (2006): 19–40.

Dunning, Thad, and Leslie Wirpsa. 2004. "Oil and the Political Economy of Conflict in Colombia and Beyond: A Linkages Approach." *Geopolitics* 9, no. 1 (2004): 81–108

Daily Independent (2007). Soldiers Kill Nine Militants in Bayelsa. Thursday, June 14 p 1 & 2 Daily Independent (2007). Two hostages Regain Freedom Thursday, June 14 pA6

Daily Independent (2007). Militants Blow up Shell Pipeline in Bayelsa Wed June 13P A1 & 2 Daily Independent (2007). 'Leave Niger Delta, Now!' Dokubo warns Foreign Oil workers Monday, June 18 pp A1 & A2

Dakurah, H., Davies, S. and Sampath, R. 2001. Defence Spending and Economic Growth in Developing Countries: A Causality Analysis. Journal of Policy Modeling. 23 (6), pp. 651 – 658. Deger, S. and Smith, R. 1983. Military Expenditure and Growth in Less Developed Countries. *Journal of Conflict Resolution.* 27, pp.335-53.

Deger, S. and Smith, R. 1985. Military Expenditures and Development: The Economic Linkages. *IDS Bulletin.* 16, pp. 49 – 54.

Deger, S. and Sen, S. 1983. Military Expenditure Spin-off and Economic Development. *Journal of Development Economics.* 13 (1 -2), pp. 67 – 83.

Deger, S. 1986. Economic Development and Defence Expenditure. *Economic Development and Cultural Change.* 35(1), pp. 179-196.

De Boeck, F. 1999A. "Domesticating Diamonds and Dollars: Identity, Expenditure and Sharing in Southwestern Zaire (1984–1997)." *Globalization and Identity*: Dialectics of Flow and Closure. ed. B. Meyer and P. Geschiere. Oxford: Blackwell, pp. 177–209. Washington, DC: United States Institute of Peace, 2007.

Gleditsch, Nils Petter. "Environmental Change, Security, and Conflict." Chester A. Crocker, Fen Osler Hampson, and Pamela Aall, (eds.). *Leashing the Dogs of War.* Washington, DC

Egunjobi, L. 2005. "Nigerian Environmental Conflict Situation: A Review of Selected Cases".

Eghosa O., Dr. Augustine Ikelegbe, Dr. Omobolaji Olarinmoye, Mr. Steven Okhonmina. Youth Militias, Self Determination and Resources Control Struggles in the Niger-Delta Region of Nigeria.

El-Kenz, A. (1996). "Youth and Violence". Stephen Ellis (ed.) *Africa Now: People, Policies and Institutions.* Portsmouth (N.H), pp. 273-287

Environmental Rights Action (1999). "The Wicked Activities of Chevron in Ilaje-land". Environmental Testimonies. No. 3. Benin: ERA.

Environmental Rights Action (2000). "The Emperor has no Clothes". Report of Proceedings of the Conference on the People of the Niger Delta and the 1999 Consortium. Port Harcourt, Nov. 24.

Fearon, J. 2005. "Primary Commodities Exports and Civil War". Journal of Conflict Resolution. Vol. 49, No. 4, pp. 483-507. DOI: http://dx.doi.org/10.1177/0022002705277544 Faini, R., Annez, P. and Taylor L. 1984. Defence Spending, *Economic Structure and Growth*: Evidence Among Countries and Over Time. Economic Development and Cultural Change. 32 (3), pp. 487-498.

Human Rights Watch. (1999). "The Price of Oil: Corporate Responsibility and Human Rights Violations in Nigeria's Oil-Producing Communities". London: HRW.

Human Rights Watch (2002). "The Niger Delta: No Democratic Dividend". Human Rights Watch. Vol. 14, No. 7, Oct. New York: HRW.

Human Rights Watch (2005). "Rivers and Blood: Guns, Oil and Power in Nigeria's River State". A Human Rights Watch Briefing Paper. New York: HRW

International Crisis Group (ICG) (2006). "Fueling the Niger Delta Crisis". Africa Report No. 118-128, September.

Imobighe, T. A. 2004. Conflict in the Niger Delta. A Unique Case or a Model for Future Conflicts in other Oil-Producing Countries? Rudolf Traub-Merz [et al.] (eds.). *Oil Policy in the Gulf of Guinea: Security and Conflict, Economic Growth, Social Development*. Washington: Fredrich Ebert Stiftung.

Imobighe, T. A.; Bassey, C. O.; Asune, J. B. 2002. Conflict and Instability in the Niger Delta. The Warri Case. Ibadan: Spectrum Books.

Isumonah, V. A. 1998. Oil and Minority Ethnic Nationalism in Nigeria: The Case

Ibeanu, O. 2000. Oiling the Friction: Environmental Conflict Management in the Niger Delta. *Environmental Change and Security Project Report*, Issue 682

Ikelegbe, A.O. 2001B. Civil Society, Oil and Conflict in the Niger Delta Region of Nigeria: Ramification of Civil Society for a Regional Resource Struggle. *Journal of Modern African Studies*. 39, (3) 437-469

Ikelegbe, A.O. 2005A. Engendering Civil Society: Oil, Women Groups and Resource Conflicts in the Niger Delta Region of Nigeria. *Journal of Modern African Studies*. Vol. 43, No.2, June. 241-270.

Ikelegbe, A.O. 2005B. Encounters of Insurgent Youth Associations with the State in the Oil Rich Niger Delta Region of Nigeria. *Journal of Third World Studies*. Vol. XXII. No.1 Spring.151-181.

Ikelegbe. 2006. Beyond the Threshold of Civil Struggle: Youth Militancy and The Militarization of the Resource Conflicts in the Niger-Delta Region of Nigeria. African Studies Monographs, 27(3): 87-122, October.

IRIN (2004). Nigeria: Militia Leader Puts Freeze on Voluntary Disarmament. 16 November.

IRIN, May 2006 Joel Bisina, "Reducing Small Arms, Increasing Safety, Security and Minimizing Conflicts in the Niger Delta Region," Paper Presented at a Roundtable Organized by African Strategic and Peace Research Group (AFSTRAG), Benin City, Nigeria, June 2003

Knight, M., Loayza, N. and Villanueva, D., 1996. The Peace Dividend: Military Spending Cuts and Economic Growth. *Policy Research Working Paper 1577*, World Bank.

Kaplan, R (1994). The Coming Anarchy. *The Atlantic Monthly*, February

Knight, M., Loayza, N. and Villanueva, D. 1996. The Peace Dividend: Military Spending Cuts and Economic Growth. *Policy Research Working Paper 1577*, World Bank.

Landau, D. 1993. The Economic Impact of Military Expenditures. *PRD Working Paper No.1138*, The World Bank.

Mason, T. David & Dale, A. Krane. 1989. The Political Economy of Death Squads: Towards a Theory of The Impact of State-Sanctioned Terror. *International Studies Quarterly*. 33: 2, June pp. 175-198

Medearis, J. (2005). Social Movements and Deliberative Democratic Theory. British *Journal of Political Science*. Vol. 53, No. 1, pg. 54

Momoh, A. 1996. Popular Struggles in Nigeria. *African Journal of Political Science*. 1:2, pp. 154-175

Musah, Abdel-Fatau and Niobe Thompson. (eds). 1999. *Over a Barrel: Light Weapons and Human Rights in the Commonwealth*. India: Commonwealth Human Rights Initiative. November, 131

NDPEHRD (Niger Delta Project for Environment, Human Rights and Development) 2004, Rivers State (Niger Delta, Nigeria): A Harvest of Gun, Small Arms Project Brief Report. Newswatch, 2004, p. 10

Obasi, Nnamdi K. 2002. Small Arms Proliferation and Disarmament in West Africa. *Progress and Prospects of the ECOWAS Moratorium*. Abuja: Atrophy Productions, pp. 74-75

Obia Vincent 2007. Dokubo – Asari an Opening for Sincere Resolution. Daily Independent Thursday, June 21 p A11

Oderemi K. (2007). Niger Delta Leaders Propose 13 Point Agenda for Lasting Peace. Sunday Punch June 10

Ojudu, Babafemi, (2006). Gun Smuggling in the Niger-Delta. IRIN, May 83

Okwu-Okafor, C. Obiora. 1994. Self Determination and the Struggle for Ethno-Cultural Autonomy in Nigeria: the Zangon-Kataf and Ogoni Problems. ASICL Proc. 6 89– 118.

Olarinmoye, O.O (2007) The Politics of Ethnic Mobilization Amongst the Yoruba of Southwestern Nigeria, Ph.D. Thesis University of Ibadan.

Olawale, I. 2003 "Youth, Culture, State Collapse and Nation-building in West Africa: The Nexus Revisited". Paper Presented at the Council for the Development of Social Science Research in Africa (CODESRIA), West African Sub-regional Conference, Cotonou, Benin

Osaghae, E.E. 1986. Do Ethnic Minorities Still Exist in Nigeria? *Journal of Commonwealth and Comparative Politics*. Vol. xxiv, No 2

Osaghae, E.E. 1995. The Ogoni Uprising: Oil Politics, Minority Agitation, and the Future of the Nigerian State. African Affairs, vol. 94

Osaghae, E.E. 2001. From Accommodation to Self-Determination: Minority Nationalism and the Restructuring of the Nigerian State. *Nationalism and Ethnic Politics*, Vol. 7, No 1

Osaghae, E.E. 2003. Explaining the Changing Patterns of Ethnic Politics in Nigeria. *Nationalism and Ethnic Politics*, Vol. 9, No 3

Osaghae, E.E. 2008. Social Movements and Rights Claims: The Case of Action Groups in Nigeria's Niger Delta. Voluntas

Oduniyi, M. (2003). "Crude Oil Theft: Bunkerers get more daring". Legal Oil News, 27 May 2003.http://www.legaloil.com/news.asp

https://www.vanguardngr.com/2017/11/fact-sheet-buhari-administrations-niger-delta-news-version/

Ogbogbo, C. B. N. 2004. *Niger Delta and the Resource Control Conflict 1960-1999*. Ph. D. Thesis. Department of History. The University of Ibadan.

Ogwuda et al. (2004). "Benin Rivers Killings: US Detectives Storm Warri to Fish out Bandits". Vanguard, Wednesday, 28 April 2004. Lagos.

Ojo, O. J. B. 2002. *The Niger Delta: Managing Resources and Conflicts*. Research Report 49. Ibadan: Development and Policy Centre (DPC).

Okonta, I., Douglas, O. 2001. Where Cultures Feasts: Forty Years of Shell in the Niger Delta. Benin: ERA/FOEN.

Onimode, B. (2001). Fiscal Federalism in Nigeria: Options for the 21st Century. Vol. 1 Research Report. Ibadan.

Onojowo, D. (2001). Of Hoodlums, North and South. Punch, Sunday, 21 October 2001. Lagos.

onosode, G. 2003. Environmental Issues and the Challenges of the Niger Delta: Perspectives from the Niger Delta. *Environmental Survey Process.* Yaba: The CIBN Press Limited.

Omonobi, K. (2004). We'll flush out these sea pirates from Niger Delta, Vows Zamani Task Force Boss. Lagos. Vanguard, Lagos, 19 June.

Owabukeruyele, W. S. 2000. Hydrocarbon Exploitation, Environmental Degradation and Poverty in the Niger Delta Region of Nigeria. Lund, Sweden: Lund University.

Transparency International. 2007. Persistent Corruption in Low-Income Countries Requires Global Action". 26 September 2007.

Ukaogo, V. 1999. Transnational Business Ethnics, Government Policies and the Crisis of Pollution and Underdeveloped in the Niger Delta. A. Osuntokun (ed.). *Environmental Problems of the Niger Delta.* Lagos: Friedrich Ebert Foundation.

Ukeje, C. (2001). Youths Violence and the Collapse of Public Order in the Niger Delta of Nigeria. *Africa Development.* Vol. 26, No. 1 and 2.

Ukeje, C., Odebuyi, A.; Sesay, A.; Aina, O. 2002. *Oil and Violent Conflicts in the Niger Delta.*

UNDP. (2000). Niger Delta Human Development Report. Garki, Abuja: UN House.

Wolf-Christian, P. 2004. "Oil Production and National Security in Sub-Sahara Africa". Rudolf Traub-Merx [et al.] (eds.). *Oil Policy in the Gulf of Guinea: Security and Conflict, Economic Growth, Social Development.* Washington: Fredrich Ebert Stiftung.

Garfinkel, Michelle R., and Stergios Skaperdas. 2000. Conflict Without Misperceptions or Incomplete Information: How the Future Matters. *Journal of Conflict Resolution* 44:792-806. Gershenson, Dmitriy and Herschel I. Grossman. 2000. Civil Conflict: Ended or Never-ending? *Journal of Conflict Resolution 44:807-21.*

Grossman, Herschel I. 1995. Insurrections. *Handbook of Defence Economics, Vol. 1,* Edited by Keith Hartley and Todd Sandler, 191-212. Amsterdam: North-Holland.

HRW (Human Rights Watch) 2005. Violence in Nigeria's Oil-Rich Rivers State in 2004, Briefing Paper, New York: HRW. February, pg. 8,

Human Rights Watch. (2005). Rivers and Blood: Guns, Oil and Power in Nigeria's Rivers State", Briefing Paper, pp. 8,

Hershleifer, Jack. 1995. Theorizing about Conflict. *Handbook of Defence Economics,* Vol. 1, Edited by Keith Hartley and Todd Sandler, 165-92. Amsterdam: North-Holland. 2000. The Microtechnology of Conflict. *Journal of Conflict Resolution 44:772-91.*

Ihori, Toshihiro. 2000. Defence Expenditures and Allied Cooperation. *Journal of Conflict Resolution. 44:853-66.*

Levine, Paul and Ron Smith. 2000. Arms Export Controls and Proliferation. *Journal of Conflict Resolution 44:884-894.*

McGuire, Martin C. 2000. Provision for Adversity: Managing Supply Uncertainties in an Era of Globalization. *Journal of Conflict Resolution. 44:730-51.*

McGuire, Martin C., and Mancur Olson. 1996. The Economics of Autocracy and Majority Rule. *Journal of Economic Literature 34:72-96.*

Olson, Mancur. 2000. Power and Prosperity: Outgrowing Communist and Capitalist Dictatorships. NEW York: Basic Books.

Schelling, Thomas C. 1966. *Arms and Influence. New Haven, CT: Yale University Press. Richards, P. 1996 Fighting for the Rain Forest: War, Youth and Resources in Sierra Leone.* International African Institute & James Curry Nigeria

Saturday Independent (2007) Supreme Court Denies Dokubo – Asari Bail; Military Intervention, not the Solution to N' Delta Crisis – Augwai June 9 pp A1 & 2

Saturday Independent (2007) Militants Announce Release Five Dokubo –
Asari Arrives Port   Harcourt today. June 16 pp A 1 & A2

Sola Adebayo. (2007) Niger Delta Crisis. Shell to sack 3,500 Sunday Punch
June 10 p11 Sunday Independent (2007) Dokubo Asari Pledges to stop
Hostage Taking, Paralyses Port Harcourt June 17 pp. 1, A2

Smaldone, J. P. 2006. African Military Spending: Defence Versus
Development? *African Security Review,* 15(4), pp. 17 – 32.

Sunday Independent (2007) Militants Release 10 Indians June 17, 2007,
pA3 Stockholm International Peace Research Institutes (SIPRI), 2011.
Military Expenditure Database 2011, accessed on 20 February 2012,
http://milexdata.sipri.org

Tarrow, Sidney 1999. Power in Movement: Social Movements and
Contentious Politics. Cambridge, Cambridge University Press.

The Midweek Telegraph, April 18-24.

Vega-Redondo, Fernando. 1996. *Evolution, Games and Economic
Behaviour.* Oxford, UK: Oxford University Press.

Wittman, Donald. 2000. The Wealth and Size of Nations. *Journal of Conflict
Resolution 44:867*

Tables
Table 1: Regional Military Expenditures (billion US$)

	1988	1990	1992	1995	1998	1999	2000	2003	2004	2005	2008	2009	2010
World Total	1441	1339	1108	983	962	980	1017	1172	1237	1288	1446	1540	1559
Africa	13.9	14.6	12.0	12.8	13.7	19.0	17.0	18.3	20.5	21.4	25.6	27.1	28.5
North Africa	3	4	4	4	5.2	4.9	4.9	6.5	7.1	7.3	9.4	10	10.6
Sub-Saharan Africa	10.6	11.1	8.0	8.5	8.5	14.2	12.1	11.8	13.5	14.0	16.2	17.1	17.9
Nigeria (billion Naira)	1.2	2.2	3.0	14.0	25.162	45.4	37.49	75.9	85.0	88.5	192.0	224.0	292
Americas	583	547	507	442	409	411	428	537	583	613	692	745	767.7
North America	549	520	482	407	374	375	389	498	542	568	637	688	707.3
Central America & the Caribbean	2.8	3.0	3.5	3.7	4.0	4.2	4.4	4.2	3.9	4.2	5.1	5.5	5.6
South America	31.2	24.4	21.1	31.7	31.7	31.8	35.2	35.1	37.4	41.1	49.4	51.8	54.8
Asia and Oceania	119	128	139	145	156	161	165	193	204	214	258	284	288
Central Asia--	-	-	0.9	0.6	0.7	0.7	0.7	1.0	1.2	1.3	2.0	2.0	..
East Asia	88.4	96.8	107	110	118	120	122	147	153	161	197	218	222
South Asia	18.3	19.3	18.5	21.5	24.0	26.9	28.0	29.6	33.6	35.2	39.6	43.6	42.6
Oceania	12.6	12.3	12.6	12.8	13.4	14.0	14.0	15.3	15.9	16.4	19.0	20.4	21.3
Europe	673	579	388	330	320	326	335	351	353	354	378	387	376
Western Europe	317	320	306	278	280	286	287	293	293	289	297	306	297
Eastern Europe	296	233	59.1	32.0	20.9	21.4	28.8	37.2	39.0	43.1	58.5	59.8	59.1
Central Europe	59.5	26.5	23.1	20.2	19.5	19.0	19.1	20.6	20.5	21.4	22.2	21.4	20.5
Middle East	52.3	70.0	62.5	52.7	62.2	62.1	71.3	72.7	77.4	85.2	93	97	98.6

Source: Stockholm International Peace Research Institutes (SIPRI) Military Expenditure Database 2011, http://milexdata.sipri.org.

Pictures

Pix 1: This is Oloibiri, Bayelsa State, the first place that crude oil was discovered in 1956 for export by Royal Shell, a Dutch multinational company.

Pix2-6: This shows the environmental pollution and degradation on the farmland and water of the oil-producing communities which have an adverse effect on their livelihood which is primarily farming and fishing. This does not only affect their livelihood and means of survival, but it also has an effect on the health of the people. According to United Nations report (http://www.theguardian.com/environment/2011/aug/04/niger-delta-oil-spill-clean-up-un), it will take 30 years and an estimate of $1 billion U.S dollars to clean up the environmental pollutions and degradation caused by the oil spills in the region. This is also one of the fundamental reasons for the crisis and violent conflict in the region by the militants.

Pix 7-9: This is when the Amnesty Programme was launched in 2011 by the Federal Government of Nigeria which gave the militants the option to surrender their weapons. This programme was initiated by the Federal government of Nigeria to put a stop to the continuing crisis in the region and to reintegrate the militants into the society so that they can live a meaning and productive life and to become responsible citizens in the country. The Amnesty Programme was estimated to have cost the Federal Government over $660 million U.S. Dollars.

www.ingramcontent.com/pod-product-compliance
Lightning Source LLC
Chambersburg PA
CBHW031513210526
45463CB00014B/2162